A LANCASTER ALPHABET
Letterforms from the Stones of the City

A LANCASTER ALPHABET
Letterforms from the Stones of the City

SIMON HAWKESWORTH

Fast Foot Press
Lancaster
www.fastfootpress.co.uk
2012

A Lancaster Alphabet: Letterforms from the Stones of the City, by Simon Hawkesworth.

First published in Great Britain in 2012 by Fast Foot Press.

British Library Cataloguing in Publication Data. A catalogue record for this book is available from the British Library.

ISBN: 978-0-9571922-0-1

Printed by Carnmor Design and Print and bound by Sanderson Bookbinders, both of Preston, Lancashire, using Fedrigoni Bodonia, Arcoprint Edizioni and Marcate papers. Set in Arno and Whitney typefaces. Designed by Fold Design: www.folddesign.co.uk.

Fast Foot Press is an independent publisher. Based in Lancaster, it develops publications relating to social history, architecture, the arts and design.

Fast Foot Press

18 Hastings Road, Lancaster, LA1 4TH

web: www.fastfootpress.co.uk - email: info@fastfootpress.co.uk

Bartlett Hall
Williamson Road, Lancaster, LA1 3PY

Alexandra Hall
Penny Street, Lancaster, LA1 1XN

...the stones of Lancaster do sometimes whisper, even yet, of rich men passed away—upon whose great prosperity some of these old doorways frowned sullen in the brightest weather...

The Lazy Tour Of Two Idle Apprentices, 1867
CHARLES DICKENS & WILKIE COLLINS

CONTENTS

PREFACE

This book is about lettering, social history and design. But it is also about the places we live in and our appreciation and connection to them. In researching the lettering on the buildings and memorials of Lancaster I began to find not only a great wealth of local design history, but also the stories behind the buildings and the people and organisations associated with them. Much of this was largely unknown to me, and even the architectural beauty and detail of many of the buildings had somehow eluded me, despite having passed by them thousands of times. Through these unfolding words, places and characters I learnt something of the work, values, hopes and fears of the former inhabitants of my adopted city. I also gained an admiration for the skill and endeavour that enabled them to create these beautiful letters, structures and designs. These discoveries have ultimately given me a greater appreciation of the city, as well as the desire to reveal it to others through this publication. These letterforms, so closely associated with the development of Lancaster, are an invitation to observe, explore and investigate the city's heritage—to wander its streets, visit the buildings, the archives and museums, or simply to look up and see the potential of this unique place. This Lancaster alphabet is a small contribution to the celebration and revelation of a remarkable city.

Simon Hawkesworth

Lancaster

2012

INTRODUCTION

This alphabet is taken from twenty-six examples of architectural and commemorative lettering found in the city of Lancaster. They represent only a small part of the large number of lettering that can be found inscribed or set in relief on the stone façades of the buildings and memorials. They are an almost forgotten aspect of Lancaster's long legacy of outstanding commercial and civic design; structures devised and constructed by architects and artisans who had a desire to express civic pride and fine craft along with the need to produce functional spaces.

Yet, despite the historic and design value of these letterforms, they remain largely unknown. Perhaps this is because they often sit above eye level, over doorways, on gable ends, or are hidden among the paraphernalia of modern advertisements and signage. Sometimes they are weathered into the stone or observable only when the correct lighting allows. But they are there, revealing the names and histories of the city's past. The recent discovery of a magnificent 1st century AD Roman funerary monument, complete with carved cavalry officer and accompanying inscription, reveals the early origins of stone-cut lettering in Lancaster. This, and the later examples of lettering, are tangible connections to the ancient histories and inhabitants of the city.

There is a remarkable variety of letterforms to be found in Lancaster. Serifs and san serifs, Roman, Gothic and cursive forms, those incised into the stone and those cut in relief. Some are beautiful, some strange, some are even crude and inelegant, but each provides an insight into the varied uses of architectural lettering, the skill of

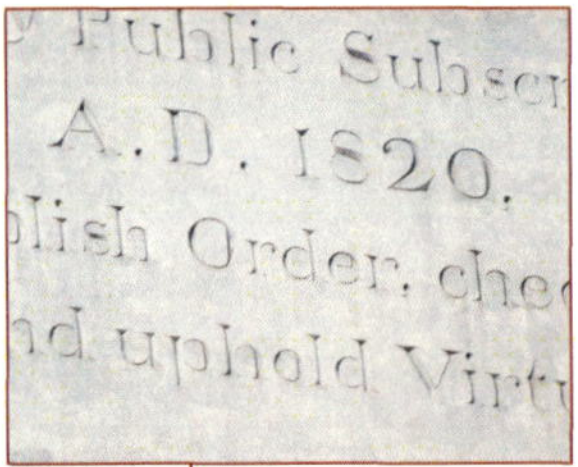

the workers who created them and the value of the built environment that hosts them.

While undoubtedly influenced by both the typographic forms and stylistic fashions of their age, many of the examples have an originality that makes them unique to Lancaster. Free from the regularity found in printed type, these hand-crafted letterforms allow the artisan great innovation. Different stylistic elements are often combined and the basic letterform modified and embellished through the mason's craft and imagination. The diversity of lettering, the quality of their construction and the stories behind each example, bear testament to the rich architectural resources and heritage of Lancaster.

For example, in one small corner of the city, in the back streets of Meeting House Lane, we find lettering that illustrates aspects of the city's social history: the development of the school system, religious and non-conformist groups, emerging mercantile and industrial enterprises and the development of public services. We also find evidence in the street names of a forgotten parliamentarian, thief and villain—one John Fenton-Cawthorne. Close by is the National Girls School that he helped establish, with its stone plaque announcing its intention to 'uphold virtue' and 'check vice'. Heading South of the city centre, and set above the entrances to the former Greaves County School, we find beautiful lettering with characteristics reminiscent of the Arts and Crafts movement and of the Art Deco period yet to come. Yards from this is a Wesleyan chapel of 1908, with intricate Blackletter inscriptions above the doorways that complement the building's Gothic features. These buildings and their lettering, though different in design and purpose, are indicative of the expanding school and church populations at this time, and of the emergence of new communities in an area that had once been outside the city's boundaries.

Among Lancaster's architectural gems is the Co-operative building on the corner of New Street and Church Street. Built in 1901 and designed by prolific local architects Austin & Paley[12], it functioned as a Co-operative department

store until its closure in the 1980s. The beautifully constructed façade is decorated with pilasters, classical motifs, geometric patterns and the Co-operative's iconic symbol of the beehive. But largely unnoticed alongside

these elements is an equally wonderful piece of design; a frieze of lettering cut into the stonework of the building that proclaims the: LANCASTER AND SKERTON EQUITABLE INDUSTRIAL CO-OPERATIVE SOCIETY LTD. The frieze is cut with exquisite skill, with letters that incorporate unusual circular protrusions, slanted letters and overlapping elements. These buildings enrich the public space and their letterforms contain stories that are locked into the stonework. They are small pockets of social history located within a few short streets and roads.

Walk just a few yards further along New Street and you will encounter the entrance to the Junior section of Lancaster Library (now the Library's Community Heritage Centre). Here, elegant lettering sits above the doorway between the expertly constructed classical architectural elements; remnants of the building's former use as a savings bank. A few streets away, on Meeting House Lane, we find a building that includes a large letter S, set high on the gable. The initial stands for Storey, a company whose impact on the industrial and architecture fabric of Lancaster still resonates today. The building, the Storey Institute, was the predecessor of the public Library, and is another of Lancaster's outstanding architectural examples. Built in 1891 as a place for technical and artistic education, it accommodated libraries, art fairs and public lectures, and remains at the heart of the city's creative industries.

From the Storey, a lane leads over Castle Hill and down on to the Quay where the derelict remnants of the city's former industrial powerhouse can be found. On a crumbling building are found three small letters–J.W.L.–that are a hybrid of Blackletter and Roman lettering, and which stand for James

Williamson, Linoleum. This was the location of Luneside Mills, once among the largest industrial sites in the world. Luneside's success furnished the Williamsons with riches and prominent political positions including Town Mayor, seats in Parliament and a place in the House of Lords. Their patronage led to the development of several key buildings and institutions in Lancaster.

Many lettering examples are commemorative, representing a desire to preserve the memory of the influential or the departed. Behind the Town Hall is the War Memorial with an inscription cut in traditional, elegant serif lettering on blocks of monumental stone, alongside bronze plaques bearing the names of the fallen. Back on Castle Hill, in a modern amphitheatre constructed from Eighteenth and Nineteenth century gravestones, lies another memorial. Long forgotten, it is dedicated to John Stirzaker, aged just twenty-one when his mother and father laid him to rest in August 1845. Walk up Moor Lane and we find the Gregson Centre, whose strip of letters across the frontage confirms its construction to the memory of Henry Gregson, MP and church benefactor. Adjoined to this is Bartlett Hall, a temperance building that commemorates (with fading letters in relief) the first Reverend of Christ Church: a collection of buildings and stone-cut details that are indicative of the intertwining relationship between the political, social and religious components of the city.

Other examples show the development in the mid-1800s of 'friendly societies' that provided benefits to their members in a time before trade unions and the Welfare State. They include the Friendly United Order of Mechanics and the Oddfellows, whose community buildings and fine memorial plaques contain secret symbols from antiquity. Some time after 1844, the word Oddfellows was removed from the name of the hall on Brock Street; by whom and for what reason, we may never know. Another story to be explored, another mystery to be uncovered.

While the city has many examples of architectural lettering from the Nineteenth century and a number from the Eighteenth and Seventeenth centuries, there are far fewer examples dating from after the 1930s. The development of painted and plastic fascias and the expansion of commercial advertisements, along with the increasingly transient function of buildings, removed much of the rationale for lettering cut in stonework. Date stones still surface from time to time and there are some fine examples of recent monumental lettering to be found, if one looks hard enough, but the lettering skill of the mason is now largely restricted to the cutting of words into a headstone. It is the longevity of lettering cut into the fabric of the city that helps us to explore these half-forgotten stories, buildings and characters. The stones of Lancaster do indeed, as Charles Dickens and Wilkie Collins wrote, 'Sometimes whisper, even yet'.

Friendly United Order of Mechanics
Nos. 2-12 Hala Road, Lancaster

LETTERFORMS

Bartlett Hall

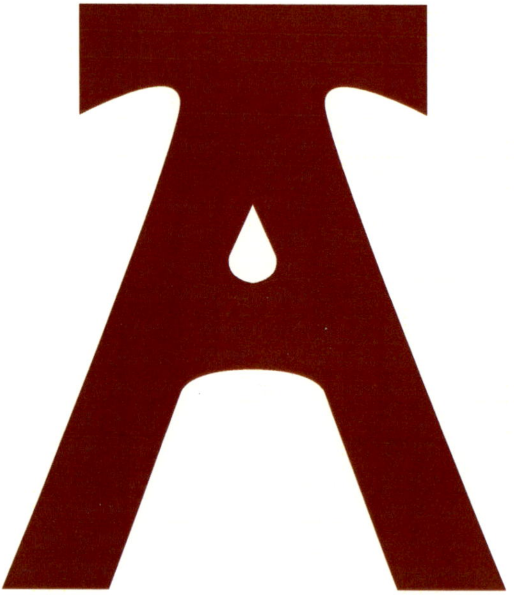

Bartlett Hall now forms part of the Gregson Centre, a popular community and arts venue on the city's Moorgate. The hall was constructed in 1912 as an extension to the original and adjoining Gregson Memorial Institute that was built in 1894 as a Temperance hall and library. Named in commemoration of the Reverent Philip Bartlett, first Vicar of nearby Christ Church (1873–1894),

1912

Williamson Road, Lancaster, LA1 3PY
Grid Reference: SD 48220 61673

the hall and church were strongly associated with the Gregson family, whose members included MPs and mayors of Lancaster. Samuel Gregson Jnr co-founded the Natural History Museum in London along with another notable Lancastrian, Richard Owen, the man responsible for giving us the word 'dinosaur'.

The letters that commemorate the construction of the hall are cut in relief and set within a plaque above the entrance on Williamson Road. The letter A shown here has a strong top bar and a beautiful rendered teardrop counter. The top bar, while rarely used in examples seen in Lancaster, is a commonly found feature in architectural lettering, and is thought to be a device designed to bridge the gap that occurs between the tapered top of the A and adjacent letters. The Bartlett letters, despite the unusual A, are quite simple in form with largely uniform stroke widths and the hint of very subtle serifs on letters such as the T and the L.

The entrance way beneath the commemorative lettering is constructed of some beautifully cut stonework, with a moulded frame and lintel sitting below a cornice. Both the lettering and the doorway appear to have suffered somewhat from air pollution, and are degraded, losing much of their original sharpness and clarity.

Telephone Exchange
Cawthorne Street, Lancaster, LA1 1TG

NCE

J. Bibby & Sons

B

While the letters found at Bartlett Hall may seem a little rudimentary, those from our next example are much more sophisticated in terms of their construction and design. This inscription identifies the firm of J. Bibby & Sons, corn merchant and miller, who commissioned this imposing five-storey warehouse and mill at Fleet Square. The letters are set within a moulded frame that sits below the Doric pediment of the

1881

Fleet Square, Lancaster, LA1 1HA
Grid Reference: SD 47600 61920
Listed Building: Grade II

building's entrance on New Road. The letters are cut in relief and have strong bracketed serifs, large full stops and an unusually intricate ampersand.

The building, constructed around 1881 from coursed sandstone, has ashlar bands at the level of each floor. It was built on the site of an earlier two-storey warehouse, and was unusual in that it had its own processing facilities for milling grain to produce animal feed and flour. The building's construction is indicative of Lancaster's connection to a global trade in grain that was occurring at the time.[10]

When Bibby and Sons relocated to Liverpool, the building was occupied by W. & J. Pye (latterly as Pye Bibby Agriculture), for whom it then served as a warehouse and mill. Pye's acquisition of larger premises on the Quay in 1918 saw the Fleet Square site then become used as offices. Pye's relocation from the centre of Lancaster in the late 1990s resulted in the building being occupied by the Lancaster and District YMCA.[28]

Most recently (2011) it has been adapted to offices and apartments, including a two-storey extension on Damside Street that includes an accompanying date stone.

YMCA

Before their relocation to Fleet Square, the Lancaster branch of the YMCA had purpose-built premises at China Street. The inscription above the doorway to this building is a wonderful example of the kind of expressive lettering that appeared during the early part of the Twentieth century. The letter C is almost the least flamboyant of the set. The concave face of the upper serif and the

1908

18 China Street, Lancaster, LA1 1EX
Grid Reference: SD 47499 61830

deeply curving bracket are perhaps the main flourishes in an otherwise simple letterform. The other associated letters are more indicative of the era with an unusual curving top bar to the letter **A**, upwardly angled bowls on the **D** and **B**, along with some accompanying subtle slur serifs. The date elements 9 and 0 are playfully intertwined and are a beautiful example of the skill of the mason who cut them. Despite the building's position on one of the busiest roads in the city, the letters remain remarkably sharp and unmarred by the passage of time and pollution from heavy traffic.

The deeply recessed doorway is flanked by pilasters that are repeated across the frontage, with the lettering sitting above a moulded semicircular pediment. A gated passageway, with a moulded arch, sits to the right of the main entrance. This is also flanked by pilasters. Sadly, parts of the building were left unused for many years and were in an increasingly poor state of repair. But at the time of writing, the premises are in the process of being renovated as student accommodation, and this fine building may once again serve to benefit the city.

Insus Son of Dodullus

This is one of the earliest examples of stone-cut lettering to be found in Lancaster. Cut around 1,900 years ago, the inscription commemorates the life and death of a cavalry officer, a member of the Roman army unit who garrisoned the military fort that once occupied Castle Hill. The inscription reads:

DIS MANIBVS INSVS VODVLLI
[...] CIVE TREVER EQVES ALAE
AUG [.] VICTORIS CVRATOR

c.75-120

Lancaster City Museum, Market Square, Lancaster, LA1 1HT
Grid Reference: SD 47610 61732

DIS MANIBVS INSVS VODVLLI
[...] CIVE TREVER EQVES ALAE
AUG [.] VICTORIS CVRATOR
DOMITIA [...]

DOMITIA [...] (TO THE SHADES OF THE DEAD. INSUS SON OF DODULLUS, CITIZEN OF THE TREVERI, CAVALRY OF THE ALA AUGUSTA, TROOP OF VICTOR, CURATOR. DOMITIA HIS HEIR HAD THIS SET UP).[2]

The funerary monument was found during the development of the area around the canal basin, and is now exhibited in Lancaster City Museum. It is an outstanding example of its type and an important artefact relating to the city's early history.

While the carving of the cavalry figure that adorns the monument is skilfully rendered, the letters themselves appear almost crude in their construction and form. These are so-called 'rustic' letterforms that originated from the everyday script of the 1st century Roman Empire. They are an interesting contrast to the grand and beautifully constructed letters that we have come to associate with the magnificent buildings of classical Rome. Traces of red dye are still visible on the stone, suggesting that the letters would have originally been painted.[2]

The devotion of the family and friends of Insus in the construction of this wonderful monument, leaves us with a tangible connection to this early citizen of Lancaster through a series of simple incisions in stone.

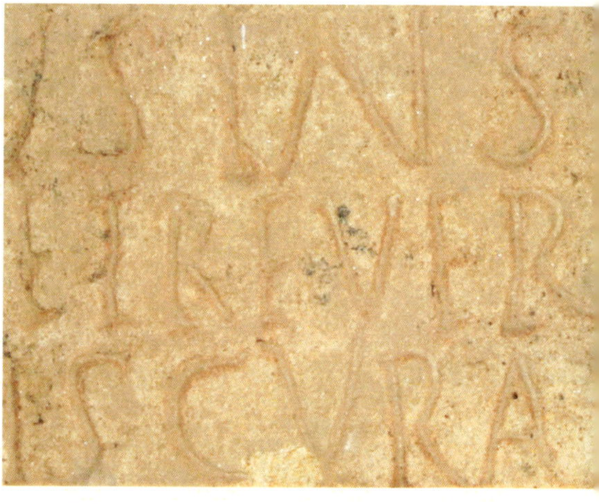

William Beckett, Grocer

From the site of the Roman fort, the route from its gatehouse came to define one the city's oldest thoroughfares, that of Church Street, and the location of our next letter. Sitting on the frontage of a row of three-storey buildings at the bottom of the street, these letterforms are some of the largest of their kind in the city. They are carved in relief within a moulded frame and are a lovely and rare example in Lancaster of a slab serif. The initials B.W.E. refer to William Beckett

1850

26–28 Church Street, Lancaster, LA1 1LH
Grid Reference: SD 47715 61812

B W. E 1850.

(1814–) and his wife, Elizabeth (nee Brade) (1812–1851).[4] In addition, there are smaller, moulded panels flanking the main one. These are without stone-cut lettering, but the faded remains of painted figures—No. 42 to the left and No. 44 to the right—are just discernible.

As early as 1844, William Beckett, (originally from Darwen in Lancashire) began his business as a grocer and tea merchant at No.43 Church Street;[18] indicating a location directly across from this building. The premises (originally Nos. 42–44, but now Nos. 26–28) were built in 1850, with the Becketts apparently both living and trading from the building. Interestingly, it was under Beckett that T.D. Smith, one of Lancaster's most noted small businessmen and grocers, was apprenticed (1853–57);[27] later establishing a string of successful shops in the area.

By 1861, the extended Beckett family was living further along Church Street (Nos. 33–34) and had expanded the business to include drapery and tailoring. The family later continued to trade in other premises within the area, including Great John Street. The building at Nos. 42–44 Church Street appears to have passed to new owners sometime before 1879. Census data from 1881[30] describes William Snr as being both a farmer of twenty-one acres and, along with his son, William Jnr, a tailor/draper. However, in 1882, records show that William Beckett Jnr filed for bankruptcy and went into liquidation,[26] though whether this was the entire business or a component part is unclear. William Jnr's younger brother, Alfred (1849–), continued to trade as a tailor in Lancaster until at least 1913.[18]

Friendly United Order of Mechanics

In addition to lettering seen in commercial and commemorative locations, some fine examples are also found on domestic buildings. The letters F.U.O.M. are cut in relief on the façade of a row of Victorian houses on Hala Road. The initials refer to the Friendly United Order of Mechanics. The Mechanics organisation appears to have been established in Lancashire around 1757 as a schism of freemasonry.[17] It was one of a number of 'friendly societies' of the period that aimed to provide, among other benefits, death and sickness relief to its members.

1874

2–12 Hala Road, Lancaster, LA1 4QJ
Grid Reference: SD 48044 59365

F.U.O.M. 1874. S

This row of six terrace properties appears to have been a small housing development undertaken on behalf of the society. It seems likely that the Friendly Order was itself a breakaway group of the earlier and more widely established Independent United Order of Mechanics, as some 500 members of the Independent Order are known to have seceded from the Lancaster organisation in 1858.[16]

The letters have stems of uniform width (described as monoline), with an unusually truncated lower arm on the letter F. The letters, along with the accompanying masonic symbols of the set square, the compass and the date of 1874, are cut with great skill and are set within a raised panel. There is an additional separate letter S found between the set square and the compass. It's been suggested that this is a Masonic symbol that stands for 'Supreme Grand' (that is, God).[17]

The function of these friendly societies was largely superseded by the development of the trade union movement in the latter part of the Nineteenth century, and by the Welfare State in the Twentieth; although Mechanics organisations can still be found today in parts of Europe, North America and the Caribbean.

Gillow & Co.

These engraved and gilded letters are set above the doorway to the original premises of the Gillow furniture company on Castle Hill. The simple title 'Gillow & Co' gives little indication as to the international renown that this company would establish by the middle of the following century. Believed to be purpose-built in 1770, this warehouse and workshop was probably designed by Richard Gillow, son of the company founder, Robert.[10] From these premises Gillow quickly developed a reputation

1770

1 Castle Hill, Lancaster, LA1 1YS
Grid Reference: SD 47485 61847
Listed Building Grade II

as a furniture designer and manufacturer of outstanding craftsmanship. Importing hardwoods from the West Indies and elsewhere (often using its own ships, built in the town's shipyards), it created furniture of the highest quality and fitted out many fine buildings in Lancaster and in other cities. It even opened a shop in London's Oxford Street in 1769.[21]

Gillow has been credited with the invention of the original billiard table and also submitted patents for the telescopic dinning table. Their renown saw reference to them in the works of Jane Austin (*Emma*), William Thackery (*Vanity Fair*) and a Gilbert & Sullivan operetta (*HMS Pinafore*). By 1881, the company had moved to a large purpose-built factory and showrooms on North Road. Gillow eventually evolved into Waring and Gillow Limited, and traded in Lancaster until 1960. The North Road premises were used for a period in the mid-1960s as the temporary site of the city's newly established university.

The letters are shallowly cut into the doorway lintel with largely uniform stroke weights and subtle bracketed serifs that have strong, blocky terminals to some of the stems. They are spaced a little unevenly but still work well. Along with the quirky, script-like ampersand, the letterforms have an almost naive feel to them.

The building is constructed from coursed sandstone with quoins and ashlar dressings. It consists of three storeys with a central loading bay that is flanked by a window. It is now used as private apartments.[10]

Oddfellows Hall

Set in a plaque on the gable end of a large three-storey building on Brock Street (now used by a furniture company), the word 'Hall' is a fine example of a slab serif with its characteristic 'blocky' or slab-like terminals. Accompanying these are contrasting date elements (giving the date of construction as being 1844) that have unusual bulbous terminals to their stems. All are expertly cut and are set within a moulded frame. What is now missing is the word 'Oddfellows', which was removed from the façade at some point after the building stopped being the meeting place for this friendly society.

1844

5–11 Brock Street, Lancaster, LA1 1UR
Grid Reference: SD 47758 61584

The Oddfellows were a benevolent and sickness relief society that was established in England in the late 1700s. In Lancaster, their benefits and activities included a widows and orphans fund, and annual events organised for its members and supporters.

One suggestion on the origin of the word Oddfellows stems from their stated aim that:

'common laboring men should associate themselves together and form a fraternity for social unity and fellowship and for mutual help'.

This was a concept so contrary to the social norms of the 1700s that the members of the organisation were seen as being somewhat peculiar or odd.[13]

In 1844, three lodges collaborated to erect the hall as a place for meeting and entertainment. It was opened in July of that year by a parade of 800 society members carrying banners and accompanied by a band. The procession marched to the Priory on Castle Hill and then back to the new hall for a celebratory dinner.[6]

The building consists of three storeys built in undressed sandstone. The ground floor originally consisted of a series of cottages, the rent from which helped to support the hall above. It was sold in 1895, with the upper floors becoming known as the Palace of Varieties (1898).[6] Later, it was used as a billiard hall and a meeting place for a number of societies and activities, before its current commercial use.

Oddfellows Hall
5-11 Brock Street, Lancaster LA1 1UR

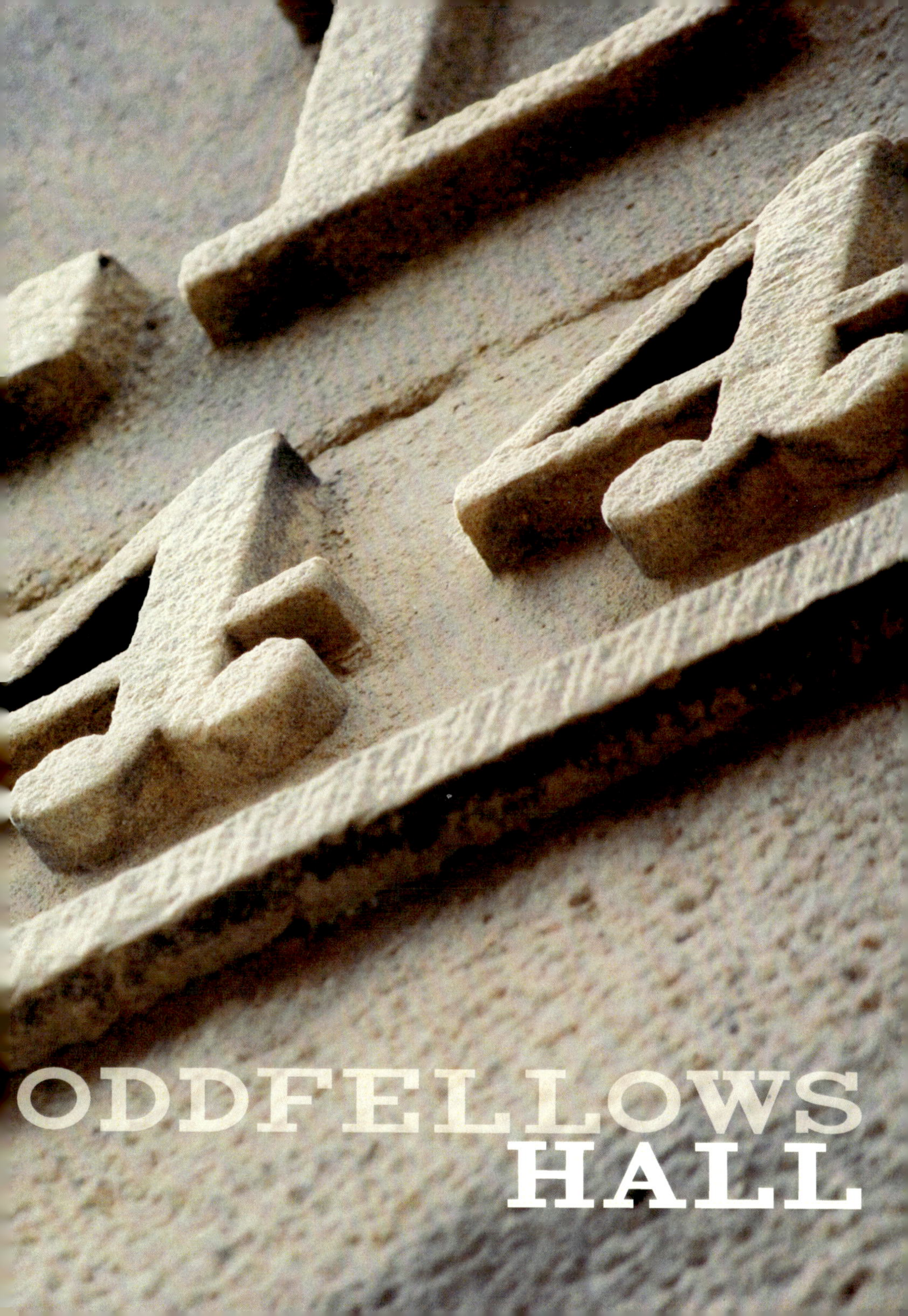

ODDFELLOWS HALL

Royal Kings Arms Hotel

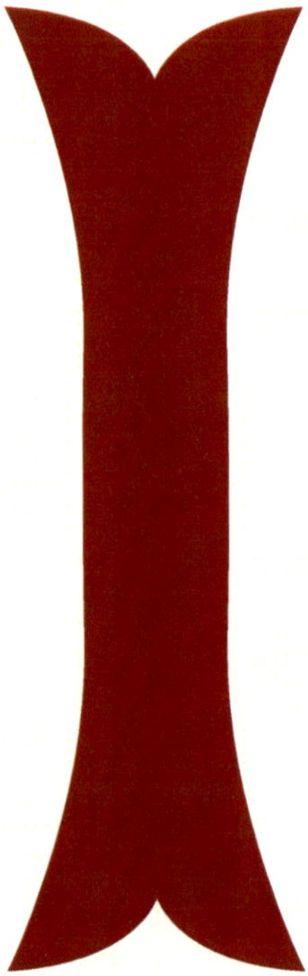

On the celebratory march from their new hall to the Priory, the Oddfellows would have passed by a large inn on the corner of King Street and Meeting House Lane, known as the Royal Kings Arms.

Originally established in the early 1600s, the current hotel was rebuilt on the site in 1879 from a design by Holtom and Connor in the Northern Renaissance style. It is constructed of sandstone and ashlar dressings with bricks at the rear. The ground floor has Tuscan pilasters above which an entablature extends along the façade on both streets. The main entrance to the hotel is found on Meeting House Lane and has a round-arched doorway with banded rustication and a scrolled pediment above. The entrance sits between pilasters that rest on high bases.[10]

High on the façade above the entrance is a plaque with lettering cut in relief. The unusual notched terminals and slightly bulging waist of the letters are an

1879

75–83 Market Street, Lancaster, LA1 1HP
Grid Reference: SD 47490 61690
Listed Building Grade II

ESTABLISHED AD 1625
REBUILT AD 1879

embellishment referred to as 'Tuscan'. The letters also have sharp, unbracketed wedge-shaped serifs that are rarely seen in the city.

In 1857, Charles Dickens and Wilkie Collins stayed together at the hotel, and there wrote the story *The Lazy Tour Of Two Idle Apprentices,* in which the Kings Arms makes an appearance:

> *I have heard there is a good old Inn at Lancaster, established in a fine old house: an Inn where they give you Bride-cake every day after dinner, said Thomas Idle.*

There is also a reflection on the ill-gotten gains of the slave trade from which Lancaster profited:

> *...the stones of Lancaster do sometimes whisper, even yet, of rich men passed away—upon whose great prosperity some of these old doorways frowned sullen in the brightest weather—that their slave-gain turned to curses, as the Arabian Wizard's money turned to leaves, and that no good ever came of it, even unto the third and fourth generations, until it was wasted and gone.*

The building remains an imposing feature of the city.

Greaves County School

Returning to the old coach road where the patrons of the Kings Arms would have rattled into Lancaster, we find an intriguing set of letterforms that were created in the period between two important styles of design.

This example of relief-cut lettering has features that express aspects of the Arts and Crafts aesthetic—'organic' elements such as the terminals with mouth-like forms (as found on the letter J), small, rounded slur serifs at the top of the stems and sensuous curves seen

1907

Greaves Road, Lancaster, LA1 4TF
Grid Reference: SD 48000 60282

SENIOR BOYS SENIOR GIRLS
JUNIOR BOYS JUNIOR GIRLS

in some of the strokes (e.g. S, Y, and R). But interestingly, it also has aspects that we often associate with the later Art Deco period—the strong contrast in weight between thick and thin strokes and the narrow letter widths, as seen in the U and N. Perhaps we are glimpsing some sort of precursor features that became more prominent in later Art Deco letterforms. The entrances for junior and senior boys and girls each had lettering cut into their respective lintels.

The building was formally the Greaves County School. It was designed by J. Mount, the Borough surveyor, and was established in 1907 with some 680 students.[19] Its construction was, in part, a response to the expanding population of the Greaves and Scotforth areas around the turn of the century,[7] as well as the establishment of publicly funded education that resulted from the 1902 Education Act. The Act saw a massive expansion in the building of secondary schools, including several seen in Lancaster from this period; a number of which, like the Greaves School, have fine lettering examples. The Greaves remained a school until 1986, when it closed and was subsequently adapted for use as private apartments.[4]

Spring Bank

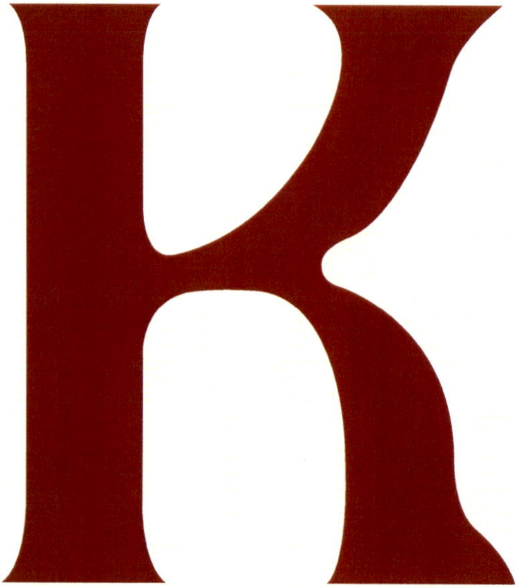

From communities that were once outside the southern limits of Lancaster, the ancient road to the North (now the A6), brings us to the area known colloquially as the 'Pointer', and the approaches to the city centre.

Here, on a row of imposing Victorian houses, are letters that exhibit a number of different design aesthetics. They have both the traditional bracketed serifs and

1881

South Road, Lancaster, LA1 4XD
Grid Reference: SD 47904 61011

variations in stroke thicknesses found in Roman letterforms, as well as the more 'organic' characteristics that feature curvaceous arms and legs (such as on the R and K).

In addition, we find one of the few examples in the city of a letter A with a broken crossbar; a design more often found in Gothic lettering. Indeed, in the flared arms of the letters accompanying the A, there is a resemblance to the rounded Gothic lettering that is usually associated with ecclesiastical buildings and scripts. The letters were cut separately and applied to the building façade as individual items, much like a set of modern signage. It's an approach that can be found in a small number of examples in the city; all naming Victorian terraces.

These substantial Victorian dwellings are constructed of ashlar sandstone with gardens to the front and rear. Between the late 1880s and early 1900s the people living there were mostly owner-occupiers, including a plumber, cabinet maker, corn merchant and bank secretary.[18, 22] A number of the buildings have recently been given over to a more varied mix of occupants that include private tenants and students.

The names of nearby locations such as Springfield Street, Springfield Barracks and Springfield Hall (since demolished, but whose estate lands were later occupied by the Lancaster Infirmary),[7] and the name of the terrace itself, suggests evidence of some sort of water source in the vicinity, though none is now discernible.

Henry Gregson Memorial

From South Road, a bridge spans the Lancaster canal. The waterway, as it curves north, skirts the rising ridge of land on which much of the eastern part of the city is built. On the old east road that leads to the high fells, is Moorgate, the site of former cotton mills, terrace housing, and a building that hosts our next letter.

The rounded protuberances seen on the terminals of these letters occur in a number of examples found in the city. They are playful embellishments to these

1889

33 Moorgate, Moor Lane, Lancaster, LA1 3PY
Grid Reference: SD 48233 61671

fine letters, with their otherwise uniform stroke widths. The letters are cut in relief within a narrow moulded frame that is recessed into the undressed stones of the building's façade.

Designed by architects Paley and Austin, the building was constructed as a Temperance hall and library in memory of Henry Gregson (1800–1885), a solicitor who became the Town Mayor (1850–51 and 1861–62). It was built with funds raised by Christ Church Vicarage, which was itself founded by Henry's father, Samuel. Samuel Gregson was the MP for Lancaster (1847) and a founder of the Natural History Museum, along with another prominent Lancastrian, the naturalist Richard Owen.

In the late 1880s, the vicar of Christ Church (Philip Bartlett) acquired the hall and let it out to the Lancaster Coffee Tavern Company; a temperance refreshment house, of which the Gregson Memorial Hall was one of several in the city.[3] In 1983, the church sold the premises to the Freehold Community Association, now called the Gregson Arts & Community Centre, but universally known as the 'Greggy'. It includes a cafe-bar, function rooms and a twenty-six seat cinema, and remains a focus for local arts and entertainment.

Mill Hall

M

A short distance from the Gregson Centre and situated on the western bank of the canal is a mid-Nineteenth century mill; one of a pair standing at either side of Moor Lane. The northern building has a recent (1989) Doric portico fronting the entrance. The letters cut into the portico—Mill Hall—are a pleasing example of how the skills of modern masons are still able to embellish the city. The letters, with their bracketed serifs and contrasting thick and thin strokes,

1989

Moor Lane, Lancaster, LA1 1QD
Grid Reference: SD 48073 61712
Listed Building Grade II

are similar to the kind of Transitional letterform that appeared in the early 1700s in England, and which were made popular by master typographers like John Baskerville (1706–1775). Indeed, the letters on the portico are like an engorged Baskerville typeface, but with more squared-off terminals on the horizontal strokes.

The mills at Moor Lane were among several built in the early to mid-1900s, as established Lancaster businesses and wealthy families exploited the upturn in the fortunes of the textile industry. The subsequent development of the mill industries had a significant impact on the increase in Lancaster's population that occurred between 1820 and 1850.[24]

The northern building may have been the site of an older industry; that of Hadwen's sailcloth factory before 1794.[15] The mill was founded in 1819 by Thomas Higgin & Company. Thomas was the second son of John Higgin Senior, Governor of Lancaster Castle. By 1828 it had become a cotton mill, and in 1846 it was taken over by Greg and Co. It was sold to the firm of Storey Brothers in 1861.[24]

The building is constructed of coursed sandstone and has vaulted brick floors carried on cast-iron beams and columns, with a roof of timber spars and purlins between sectional cast-iron trusses. It has five main storeys and includes a basement and an attic.[10]

Storey Brothers operated the mill until it closed in 1975.[24] In 1989, the mill was developed as student accommodation. The modern entrance was added by the architects Charles B. Pearson Son & Partners as part of the development. The conversion of the mill to student accommodation is indicative of the importance of the education sector for Lancaster's economy.

Junior Library

N

Storey Brothers—one of a number of influential industrial dynasties that became established in the mid-1800s in Lancaster—had a major impact, not only on commerce, but on education and the establishment of Lancaster's first public library.

A number of libraries were set up in Lancaster before the 1932 development

1932

New Street, Lancaster, LA1 1HY
Grid Reference: SD 47587 61789
Listed Building Grade II

of the main Public Library. By around 1870, Lancaster had nine different libraries. The Quaker library of 1695 on Meeting House Lane is believed to have been the first. Others under the auspices of local societies were later established in places such as coffee houses and 'newsrooms'. The first to be truly accessible to the wider public was founded in the Mechanics Institute around 1824. This was later transferred to the Storey Institute when it replaced the Mechanics Institute on the same site. Expanded to some 14,000 titles, the Storey collection became Lancaster's first public library.[23] Attempts to establish a truly public Library in Lancaster was not without contention, being defeated twice in Council in 1858 and 1860, with the Storey collection not established until 1892.[1]

The Junior Library is situated on New Street and was opened on the 4th May 1932. The premises was originally built in 1823 as the Lancaster Savings Bank (closed in 1889). It was remodelled by the architect H.A. Paley in 1848,[14] and then again in 1892, when it was redesigned for use by the Post Office.

The façade and doorway have an impressive array of architectural features. The doorway is flanked by pilasters and has a pediment with dentil mouldings. Above this is a line of Greek key decoration that runs across a course of the ashlar stonework. To the side of the pilasters are pairs of Ionic columns supporting an entablature and cornice, and which are flanked by additional pilasters.

The original architectural drawings (made in 1931 by Borough Surveyor Frederick Hill) show how the frontage was adapted to include a Doric pediment above the doorway, along with the new mouldings and ornamentation. Behind the columns that flanked the doorway are pairs of tall windows.

The lettering for what was previously the Junior section of the Public Library is cut in relief above the doorway and

set in a moulded frame. These expressive letterforms of the 1930s seem very much of their time. They are elegant with hints of the Art Deco aesthetic (the contrasting stoke widths, the somewhat condensed form and the low set crossbar of the letter A) though without some of the more exaggerated features and almost shocking modernism that was associated with that design movement.

Interestingly, the design of the lettering shown on the architectural drawings appears to be only a guideline: an initial drafting to be crafted by the stonemasons into the beautiful examples that we see today. Even the exact form of the Library name is unfinished, with the final version becoming 'Juniors' rather than the originally proposed 'Juveniles'.

The Junior Library now houses the Library's Community Heritage Centre with an excellent collection of reference material and historical documents.

An illustration of the original frontage of the building before remodelling to accommodate the new Library.

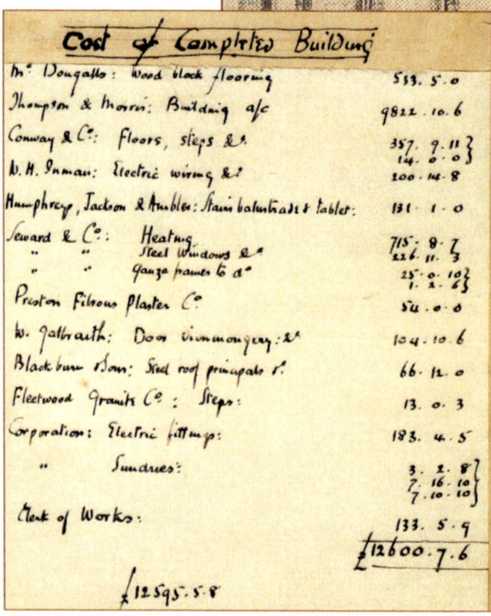

Cost of Completed Building

Mc Dougalls: Wood block flooring	533. 5. 0
Thompson & Morris: Building a/c	9822. 10. 6
Conway & Co: Floors, steps &c	357. 9. 11 14. 0. 0
W. H. Inman: Electric wiring &c	200. 14. 8
Humphrey, Jackson & Ambler: Stairs balustrade & tablet:	131. 1. 0
Seward & Co: Heating	715. 8. 7
" " Steel Windows &c	226. 11. 3
" " Gauze frames to do	25. 0. 10 1. 2. 6
Preston Fibrous Plaster Co	54. 0. 0
W. Galbraith: Door ironmongery: &c	104. 10. 6
Blackburn & Sons: Steel roof principals &c	66. 12. 0
Fleetwood Granite Co: Steps:	13. 0. 3
Corporation: Electric fittings:	183. 4. 5
" Sundries:	3. 2. 8 7. 16. 10 7. 10. 10
Clerk of Works:	133. 5. 9
	£12600. 7. 6

£12595. 5. 8

A list of the trades attending to various aspects of the project, along with an estimate of costs totalling some £12,600.

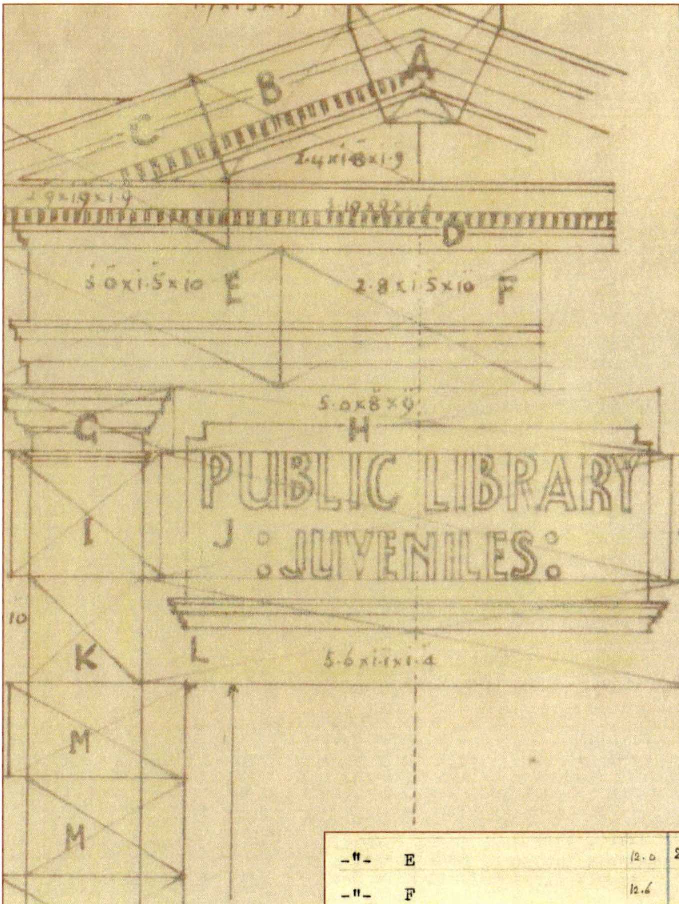

These architectural drawings show the reworked doorway to the Junior Library with the original title to the entrance being 'Juveniles' rather than the final 'Juniors'.

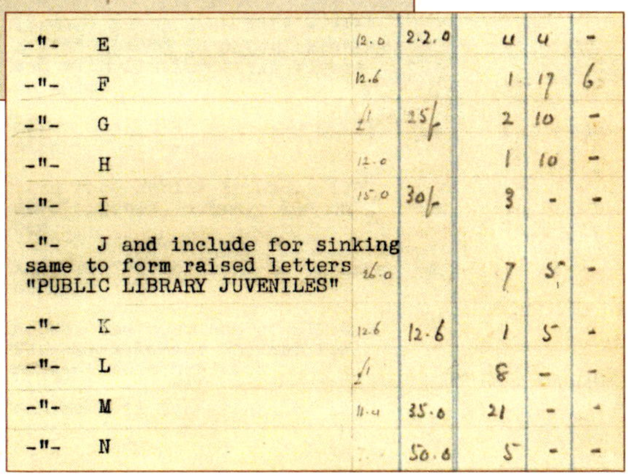

-"- E	12.0	2.2.0	4	4	-
-"- F	12.6		1	17	6
-"- G	/!	25/-	2	10	-
-"- H	12.0		1	10	-
-"- I	15.0	30/-	3	-	-
-"- J and include for sinking same to form raised letters "PUBLIC LIBRARY JUVENILES"	26.0		7	5	-
-"- K	12.6	12.6	1	5	-
-"- L	/!		8	-	-
-"- M	11.4	35.0	21	-	-
-"- N		50.0	5	-	-

Details from the architect's drawings show how the lettering above the doorway was constructed by cutting into, or 'sinking' the stonework to produce the raised lettering.

(Documents courtesy of Cultural Services, Lancashire County Council)

> ‘
> These letterforms... are an invitation to explore, observe and discover; to investigate the city’s heritage... to wander its streets, visit the buildings, the archives and museums, or simply to look up and see the potential of this unique place.
> ’

This map of Lancaster is constructed from the lettering found on over a hundred architectural and commemorative examples found in the city. It also incorporates literary elements associated with Lancaster (both historic and contemporary), the names of principle parts of the city, and fragments found in ephemeral printed items relating to many of the buildings.

River Lune
LUNE
Greyhound Bridge
Skerton
St Johns Church
STOREY INSTITUTE 1891
LIBRARY
MARKET
REBUILT 1930
Westbourne Terrace
OWEN HOUSE
GIRLS GRAMMAR SCHOOL
Boys Grammar School
Lancaster
ABRAHAM HEIGHTS
I came to Lancaster
George Fox
1652
Dallas Road
Dalton Square
Lancaster Royal Infirmary
BOWERHAM PRIMARY SCHOOL
St Thomas
Michael Murphy
I have heard there is a good old Inn at Lancaster

National Girls School

O

While improved public access to learning was being established at the nearby Mechanics Institute during the early part of the Eighteenth century, education for most young women in Lancaster at this time remained limited, with schools that largely acted to prepare them for domestic service.[15]

Our letter O is from an inscription found on one such institution from this period—the former National Girls School on High Street. The letters are set within a plaque on the gable end of the building and have fine, sharp bracketed serifs, with upper case letters such as

1820

High Street, Lancaster, LA1 1LA
Grid Reference: SD 47504 61566

the S and Y displaying curling strokes. The bowls of many of the letters could be described as 'stout': being broad and full in form. Other letters such as the P, have abruptly angled terminals to their descenders. The sharp serifs and vertical axis of the letter O for example, are characteristics found in so-called Transitional typeforms that appeared in the late 1700s. It is a beautiful example, full of flourishes and idiosyncrasies, but undermined somewhat by the rather dull stone plaque that holds it.

The land for the school was donated by John Fenton-Cawthorne (1753–1831) of nearby Meeting House Lane.[5] Known for his unpleasant disposition, he is among Lancaster's more colourful characters. He was returned as Lancaster's MP in 1806 despite being court marshalled by his regiment in 1796 for fraud. Mounting debts and the lack of heirs saw Fenton-Cawthorne's estate auctioned off after his death. His beautiful town house was later demolished to make way for the new Post Office, with only the portico being salvaged and then installed at the entrance to gardens at the rear of the Storey Institute.

BUILT BY PUBLIC SUBSCRIPTION
A.D. 1820 TO ESTABLISH ORDER,
CHECK VICE AND UPHOLD
VIRTUE. NATIONAL SCHOOL
FOR GIRLS

The school—constructed in plain domestic design and faced with ashlar sandstone—was completed in 1821 and opened under the Headship of Miss Mary Anne Hannibal.[9]

Absorbed into the elementary school system in 1903 as a result of the 1902 Education Act, the school was later used by the voluntary sector.

Primitive Methodist Church

At the same time that the School on High Street was being built, Methodism, which had seen the secession of groups such as the Primitive Methodists (1807), was beginning to undergo a reconvergence of credo among the various schisms. But for a further hundred years, groups like the 'Primitives' continued to function as independent churches. By 1895, the local Primitive Methodists—previously meeting at premises in the unusually named 'Under the Gardens'

1895

Moor Lane, Lancaster, LA1 1QH
Grid Reference: SD 48008 61727

PRIMITIVE METHODIST CHURCH A.D. 1895

at Damside[11]—had founded the new building on Moor Lane; also known as the Ebenezer church, and built in the neo-Gothic style.

This church has one of the few examples of Blackletter lettering found on buildings in the city, with the highly decorative letters being inscribed above the great double doors on Moor Lane. The lowercase letters are a form known as Textura, a style derived from the script of illuminated manuscripts. However, the capitals are unusual, being more like the rounded form of Blackletter, and they have embellishments, including lobed terminals to the stems, and in the case of the letter A, an extra middle crossbar. It's an example of the flair and individuality shown in lettering found in the city, with different styles being used together. The inscription has some additional letter spacing that not only acts to frame it better within the space provided, but also helps with the readability (compare this with the tightly spaced inscription on the Greaves Methodist Church—the letter T in this alphabetical series). Sadly, the final part of the Primitive Methodist inscription has weathered badly and is corroding to the point of being almost illegible.

In 1932, the Primitive Methodists joined with the Wesleyan Methodists and the United Methodists to form the Methodist Church of Great Britain. The Moor Lane building stopped being used as a church after 1964.[10] In the 1990s, it was converted to function as the Youth Arts Centre of the Dukes Playhouse, also located on Moor Lane.

Queen Square Medical Practice

In contrast to the elaborate Gothic lettering on the Primate Methodist Chapel, this example represents a return to the Roman serif letters that are associated with classical architecture and the world of the printed word.

A rare example of stone-cut lettering to have been commissioned in the city in

2001

2 Queen Street, Lancaster, LA1 1RP
Grid Reference: SD 47655 61428
Listed Building Grade II

recent years, this large plaque announces the medical practice that is located in a former Georgian house. The strong serifs and the contrasting widths of the strokes are beautifully worked and provide another example of the enduring skill of local masons.

The serif and stroke features, as well as the tail of the Q, have characteristics similar to those found in typefaces such as Times New Roman (1931) and Plantin (1913). These have Transitional characteristics that include a high contrast between stroke widths and the vertical axis seen in letters such as the O and the Q. The lettering is accompanied by a carving of the 'Rod of Asclepius': the serpent and staff symbols associated with medicine.

The surgery is contained within a large Georgian house that was built between 1767 and 1799. The building, constructed of sandstone ashlar and originally double-fronted with five bays and a central doorway, was altered during the Nineteenth century and partly demolished in the 1930s during the widening of the main road. As a result, only the two right-hand bays of the façade remain. Below the gutter there is a moulded eaves cornice.[10]

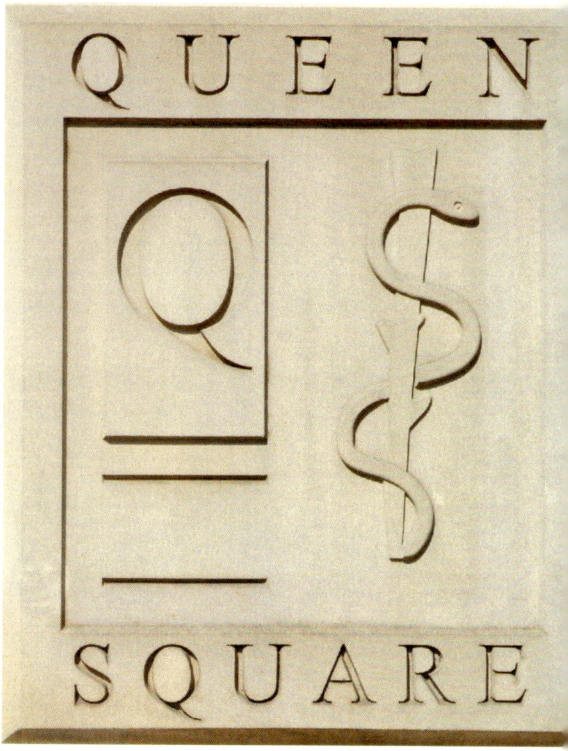

Alexandra Hall

Crossing over the road from the medical centre, we step back in time around a hundred years and find a design full of elaborate flourishes that is markedly different from the simplicity of the Roman lettering used for the letter Q.

Designed by architects Austin and Paley in a Northern Renaissance style, this three-storey building, which

1902

Penny Street, Lancaster, LA1 1XN
Grid Reference: SD 47749 61310
Listed Building Grade II

accommodates both the Alexandra Hall and Alexandra Hotel, is constructed of sandstone ashlar and stands at the point of Penny Street and Thurnham Street. It has a wealth of architectural features that includes three bands of coloured or moulded stonework running across the façades; a moulded element between the ground and first storeys, a sill band with cornice at the second storey, and twin bands of red sandstone across the third. All of the windows have segmental heads and there is a two-storey bay window on Thurnham Street with rusticated segmental lintels. Both façades have Dutch gables flanked by octagonal turrets and windows set between pilasters beneath a segmental cornice.[10] On Penny Street, on the first floor under a low strapwork gable, is a mullioned and transomed window with a stone balcony.

The façade to Penny Street has two entrances. The one to the right has an ironwork canopy bearing the name ALEXANDRA HOTEL in stained glass, while above the left hand entrance and cut in relief into the stonework, are the words ALEXANDRA HOTEL and the date of 1902. This stone-cut lettering is heavily influenced by the aesthetics of Art Nouveau, with playful forms and curves that have a strong 'organic' style. The letters have stems and legs that are 'pinched' at the waist and have wedge-shaped terminals. The letter R also has an unusual pointed bowl. The initial A of Alexandra has bulbous stems and arm terminals, while the other letter As have slur serifs at the apex. The letter D has, in addition, an unusual semi-open bowl with the downward stroke ending in another bulbous terminal.

The building, including the former hall and hotel, is currently used as both a bar and as student accommodation.

Storey Institute

Ten years before the construction of the Alexandra Hall and Hotel, Austin and Paley were to design one of their most outstanding buildings in the form of the Storey Institute.

The unusual, large letter S (for Storey Brothers) shown here with its lobed and bifurcated terminal endings, is cut in relief on the roof pediment of the Institute. It is a simple but bold statement from a family business that had an immense influence on Lancaster; not

1891

Meeting House Lane, Lancaster, LA1 1TH
Grid Reference: SD 47420 61710
Listed Building Grade II

only through the commercial importance of their factories (producing table baize and oil cloth) but in the architectural and cultural impact of their industry and patronage.

Construction of the Storey Institute began in 1887 under the auspices of Thomas Storey (1825–1898) and was completed in 1891.[14] The institute is designed in a Jacobean Revival style, and constructed of sandstone ashlar with ashlar dressings, slate roofs, curved gables and tall chimneys. Situated on a corner site (originally occupied by the Mechanics Institute) it has a domed octagonal turret at the junction of the two façades. On the side facing Meeting House Lane is a doorway, to each side of which are columns with beautiful strapwork decoration supporting an entablature. The elaborate gable has, in addition to the large letter S, cornices, finials and pilasters rising from first floor level.[10] On this side is a central oculus set in the gable and a first floor plaque engraved with: IN HONOREM VICTORIAE REGINAE NOSTRAE, MDCCCLXXXVII (IN HONOUR OF OUR QUEEN VICTORIA, 1897). While these letters exhibit the lobed and bifurcated terminals of the large letter S, they are less elaborate in their ornamentation.

The Storey is a remarkable and historically important building, having been a centre for learning and the arts since its inception. The Storey, and its immediate predecessor The Mechanics Institute, had several renowned scientists among its staff and patrons. Perhaps most notably these included: William Whewell (mineralogist who coined the term 'scientist' and recommended the terms 'anode' and 'cathode' to Michael Faraday), Edward Frankland (chemist and father of the concept of Valency, and who is credited with inventing the idea of the chemical bond) and William Turner (anatomist).[20]

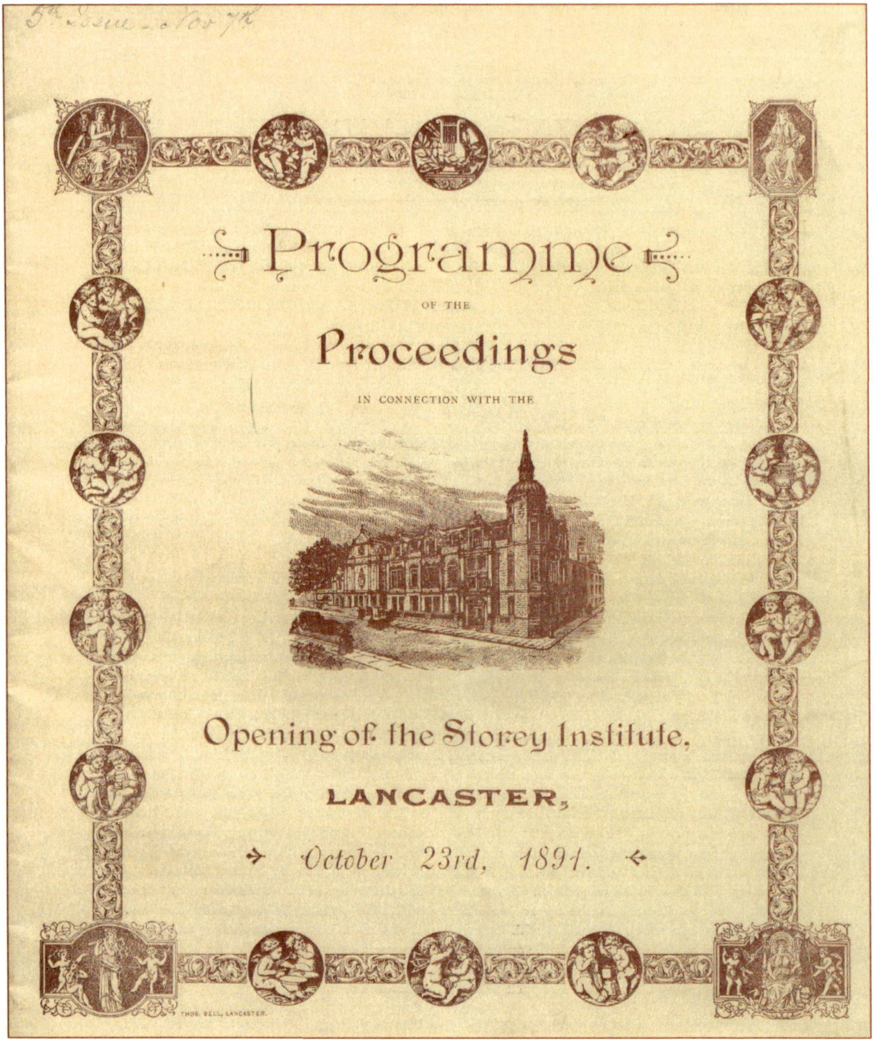
5th Issue – Nov 7th

Programme

OF THE

Proceedings

IN CONNECTION WITH THE

Opening of the Storey Institute,

LANCASTER,

October 23rd, 1891.

THOS. BELL, LANCASTER.

Programme of the Proceedings in Connection with the Opening of the Storey Institute, Lancaster. October 23rd, 1891. Printed by Thomas Bell, Lancaster (Courtesy of Cultural Services, Lancashire County Council).

One of the ornamental pillars flanking the entrance to the Storey Institute on Meeting House Lane.

Greaves Methodist Church

At the start of the Twentieth century, as institutions such as the Storey responded to the educational and commercial demands of the population, Wesleyan Methodism ministered to a growing congregation in the expanding parts of Lancaster. In these areas the Wesleyan movement established new churches, of which the Greaves was one; being constructed to a design by Stanley Wright (Mayor of Morecambe).[23]

This example of Blackletter is an extract taken from Psalm 100 and is cut in relief above the twin entrances of the building. The complex letterwork can be difficult to decipher, with the letter T being among the easiest to distinguish.

1908

Scotforth Road, Lancaster, LA1 4TE
Grid Reference: SD 47999 60327

ENTER INTO HIS GATES WITH THANKSGIVING AND INTO HIS COURTS WITH PRAISE

This is a form known as Textura, which has an almost calligraphic style as one might find in the text of illuminated manuscripts. It's an interesting example of how Blackletter, associated with ecclesiastic writing since the Twelfth century, was retained as a style of choice for architectural lettering in many churches into the Twentieth century, at a time when Roman lettering was used in almost every other context. It is also, of course, in keeping with the building's neo-Gothic design. It has a tower seventy-six feet high and is constructed of ashlar sandstone with gritstone dressings.[23]

A ceremony for the laying of the foundation stone occurred on the 14th October 1908 and was attended by, among others, Rev. W.J. Chant (the new Church Superintendent) and Councillor Wilson (Mayor of Lancaster). A bottle was placed beneath the foundation stone containing a plan, a magazine, a copy of the appeal statement, a circular announcing the ceremony, newspapers, a list of trustees, a photograph of the builder and his workmen and some coins.[23] The building was completed in October 1909 and remains in use today as a Methodist church.

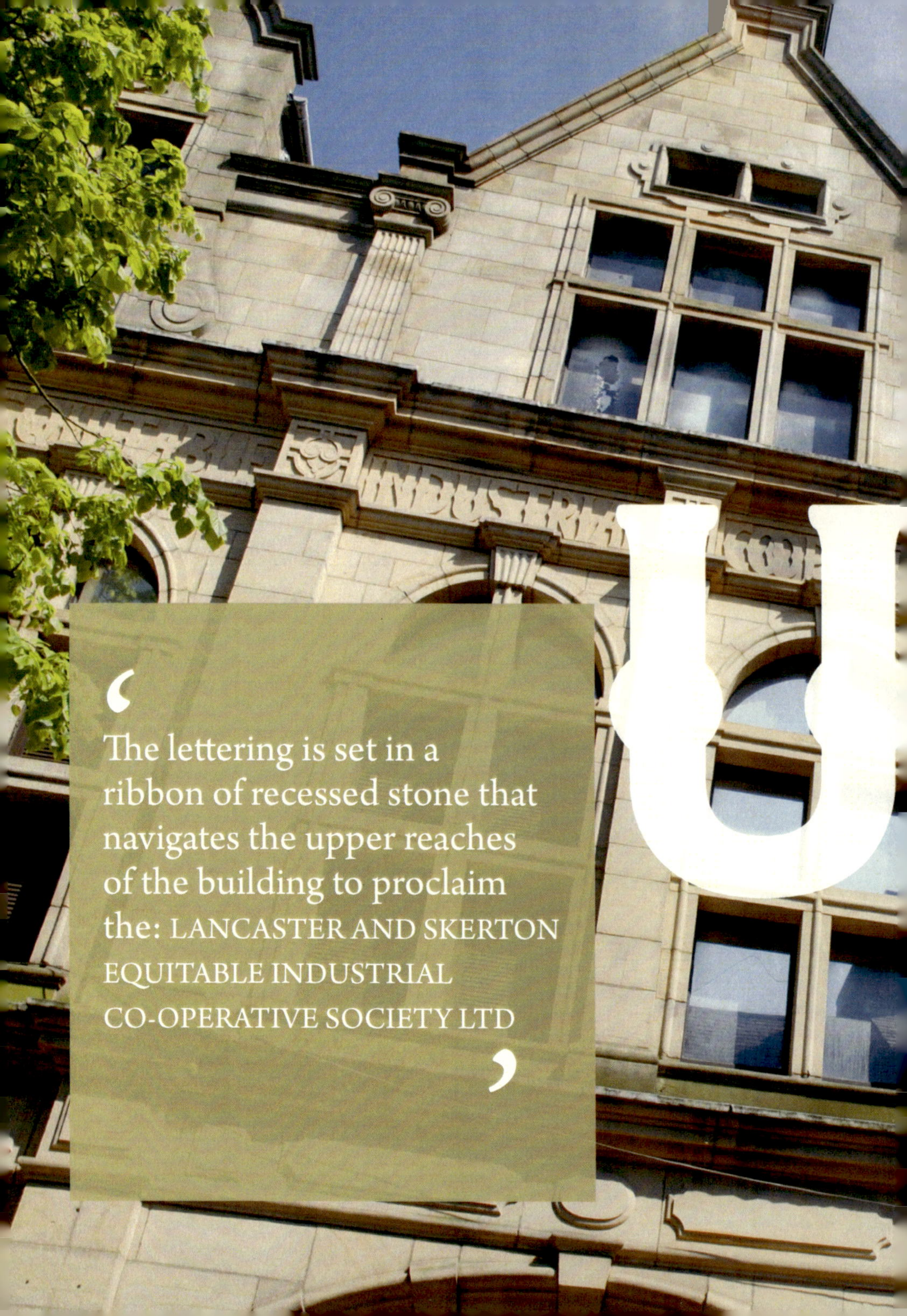

> The lettering is set in a ribbon of recessed stone that navigates the upper reaches of the building to proclaim the: LANCASTER AND SKERTON EQUITABLE INDUSTRIAL CO-OPERATIVE SOCIETY LTD

Co-operative Store
47-53, Church Street, Lancaster, LA1 1EG

Co-operative Society

U

From the modest scale of lettering found above the doors of the Greaves Methodist church, we come to a magnificent frieze running across the entire face of this impressive building. The lettering is set in a ribbon of recessed stone that navigates the upper reaches of the building to proclaim the: LANCASTER AND SKERTON EQUITABLE INDUSTRIAL CO-OPERATIVE SOCIETY LTD. The letters, cut with great skill, have unusual

1901

47–53, Church Street, Lancaster, LA1 1EG
Grid Reference: SD 47620 61800
Listed Building Grade II

circular protrusions on their stems, slanted letter As and overlapping elements. The design and execution of both the lettering and the building are indicative of the growing strength and confidence of the local Co-operative movement at this time. Functioning as a department store, it included a bank, meeting hall, library and cinema.[7] Sadly, the internal structure of the original building was demolished in the 1980s, leaving the façade to Church Street and New Street as the last remnant of the original structure.[8]

Designed by architects Austin and Paley in a Free Northern Renaissance style,[14] the building is constructed of sandstone ashlar with a canted corner bay decorated in strapwork. Below the bay is a tall semicircular oriel dated 1901 that includes more strapwork supporting a panel carved with a Lancashire rose. Behind and above this is a cross-window between a pair of Ionic pilasters, whose entablature carries an ornate Ionic aedicule. This is flanked by scrolls and capped by a segmental pediment, beneath which is a frame containing the beehive symbol of the Cooperative Society. The ground floor has moulded segmental arches with alternately projecting voussoirs, which are carried on half-octagonal piers that have banded rustication.[10] The building and its accompanying lettering and ornamentation are wonderful examples of the outstanding skills of the artisans and architects who designed and constructed them. It is a treasure to be valued and celebrated.

Claremont View

From the unique letterforms of the Co-operative building we move to a design with firm roots in typographic and lettering tradition. Sitting on the frontage of a row of Victorian houses, and accompanied by flower and leaf motifs, is the name of the terrace along with the date 1879. These letterforms are carved in relief and are of a design known as 'Clarendon'. It was a lettering style widespread in Britain from the 1820s onwards, but there are few examples found in Lancaster. This example has strong bracketed serifs, though the contrast between thick and thin strokes is unusually slight for this type of letter.

1879

Bowerham Road, Lancaster, LA1 4AA
Grid Reference: SD 48341 60691

The accompanying date numbers 1 and 7 have embellishments in the form of unusual bulges in the middle of their upright stems.

The houses in this area were constructed between the 1870s and 1890s, a period that saw Lancaster undergoing an economic boom as major employers such as Williamson, Storey and the Lancaster Wagon Company expanded their businesses. The up-turn in commerce resulted in an increase in house building to accommodate the growing industrial workforce.

Claremont View (a row of two-storey, stone-fronted terraced houses with basements, small front gardens and yards to the rear) is indicative of the type of property produced at this time; accommodating households that by the late 1890s included a printer, carpenter, tailor, manager and foreman.[18] The terrace was among the first to be built in the area known as Bowerham, one of the expanding outer parts of the city. The sandstone used in the construction most likely came from one of several quarries that are found close by.

Luneside Mills

The letter W has Blackletter elements in its joined stems and pointed spurs, but the associated J and L of the monogram (James Williamson, Linoleum) have features closer to Roman lettering. It is another example of the amalgamation of different styles found in architectural lettering in the city.

The letters, along with Lancaster's coat of arms, are set above the door of a derelict industrial building on St George's Quay. This is the site of Luneside Mills. It was built in 1875 by the Williamson family and was once one of the largest industrial complexes in the world. It was the powerhouse of a business founded initially on the

1875

New Quay Road, St. George's Quay, Lancaster, LA1 5SW
Grid Reference: SD 46971 62307

invention of 'table baize' (a type of oil cloth), and later the manufacture of linoleum floor cloth. A publicity article of 1894 stated:

> *The present undertaking constitutes the largest manufactory of its class in the world; and further, we may say, without any fear of contradiction, that the mammoth works on the banks of the Lune, at Lancaster, are the most extensive in the universe, that are owned and controlled solely by one individual.* [25]

The Williamsons had an enormous impact on Lancaster, shaping its employment, industry and transport, and their power and wealth allowed them to have a significant impact on the economic and political life of the city. This manifested itself in arrogance and exploitation, as well as generosity and a patronage that led to several key buildings, landmarks and institutions (the Town Hall, Royal Infirmary, Ashton Memorial, Williamson Park, school and hospital expansions). Between them, James and his son obtained the positions of High Sheriff, MP, and Mayor of Lancaster. James Jnr was made a Baronet in 1895, becoming Lord Ashton.

Production ceased at Luneside Mills around 1999, after a long decline in the face of economic downturn and overseas competition. With much of the site demolished or derelict there is now little to show of this once great company.

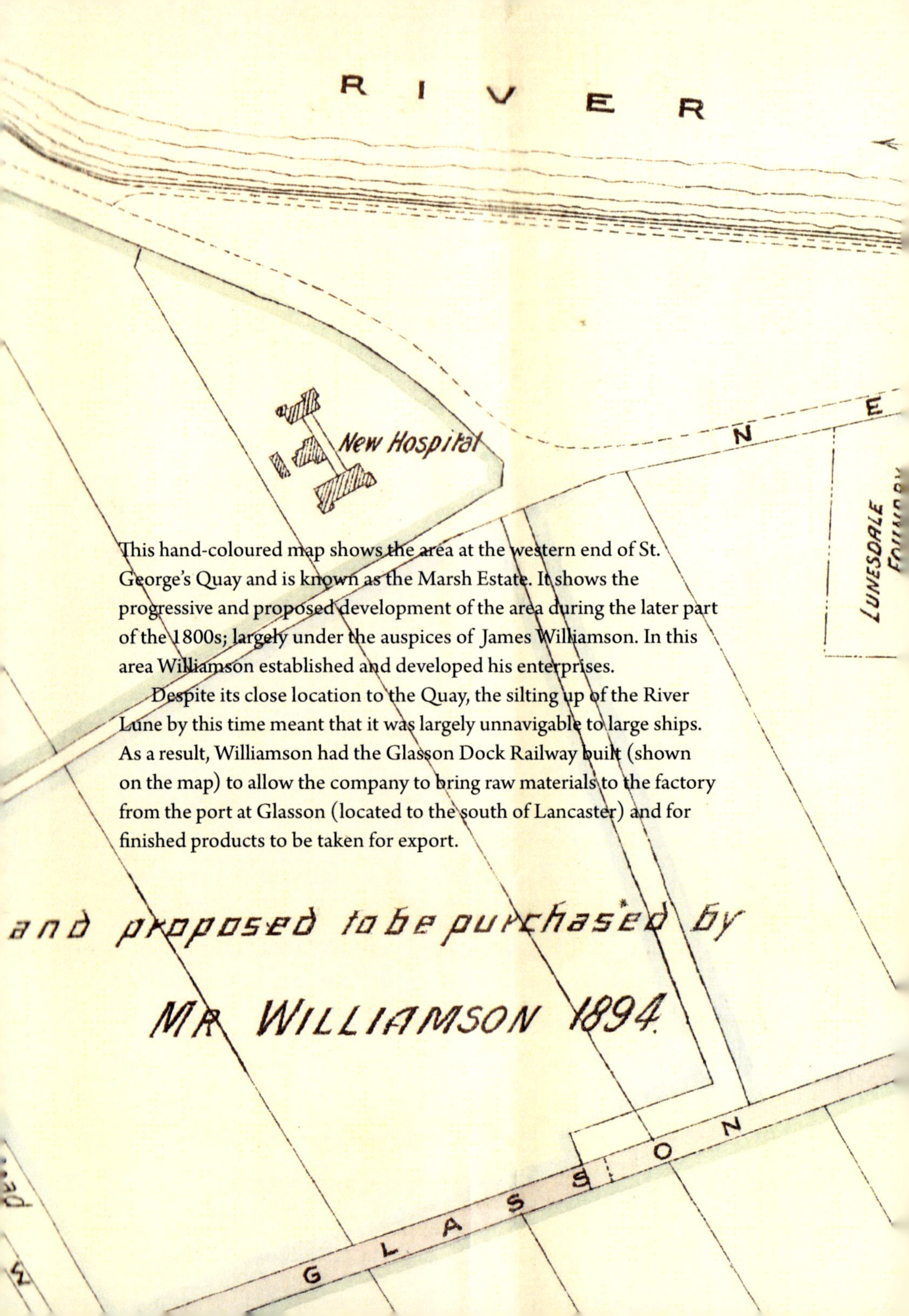

This hand-coloured map shows the area at the western end of St. George's Quay and is known as the Marsh Estate. It shows the progressive and proposed development of the area during the later part of the 1800s; largely under the auspices of James Williamson. In this area Williamson established and developed his enterprises.

Despite its close location to the Quay, the silting up of the River Lune by this time meant that it was largely unnavigable to large ships. As a result, Williamson had the Glasson Dock Railway built (shown on the map) to allow the company to bring raw materials to the factory from the port at Glasson (located to the south of Lancaster) and for finished products to be taken for export.

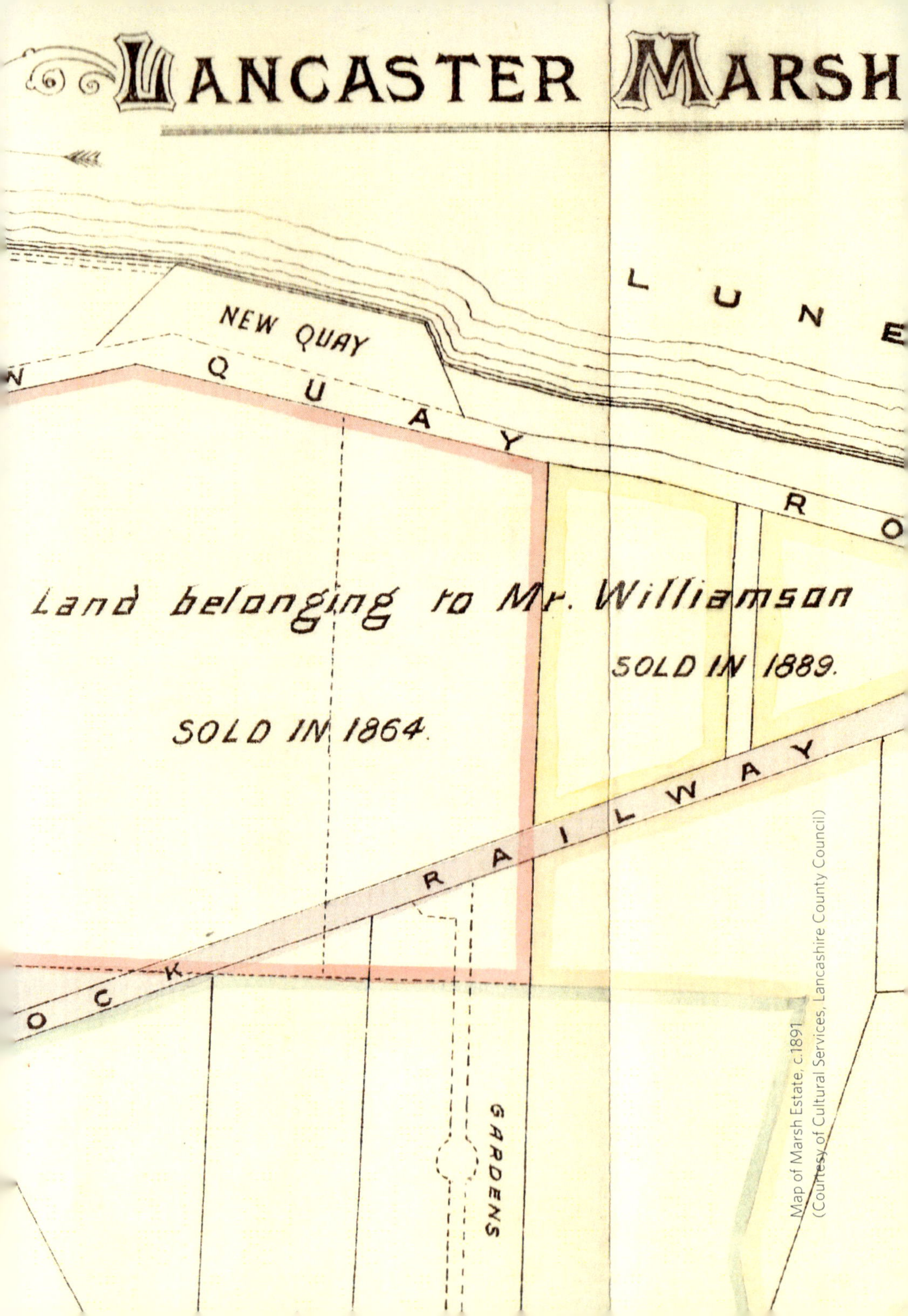

Map of Marsh Estate, c.1891
(Courtesy of Cultural Services, Lancashire County Council)

Telephone Exchange

X

From the dilapidated industrial archaeology of the Quay, a narrow lane runs up and over Castle Hill. Passing the Storey Institute and crossing Meeting House Lane, it brings us to the back streets that lead behind the Post Office (built in 1923).

Accompanying the Post Office is the Telephone Exchange. The lettering that adorns the entrance to this early 1950s Modernist building is a wonderful

1952

Cawthorne Street, Lancaster, LA1 1TG
Grid Reference: SD 47497 61580

example of san serif letterforms. These letters are beautifully designed and constructed, running in a deep frieze that is located on a low wall to the right of the entrance on Cawthorne Street. The letters are without serifs, with even, monoline stems and strokes. The proportions of the letters, their clean lines and the simplicity of their design, speak of modernity, technology and the Modernist aspirations of the building they are associated with. In addition, there is the Royal Cipher, G.R. 1952 (George VI), situated above the doorway to the left of the building name. In contrast to the serifs, these letters are cut in a cursive form.

The building of three storeys is constructed of ashlar sandstone that has a particularly warm, honey colour. The large windows, which are set regularly along each storey, have their original Crittall frames. Behind, and to the right of the two-storey entrance block, is an additional narrow window that spans the three storeys, and provides natural light to the stairwell. It is one of the few examples of Modernist architecture in Lancaster.

The building remains associated with the telecommunications industry, being used today by British Telecom plc.

War Memorial

Another example of skilfully cut letters, though of a different style, are those found on the war memorial that stands in a small garden of remembrance beside the Town Hall. Commemorating the dead of the two world wars and of the Korean War, the letters are expertly incised, with finely balanced lines that are v-cut into the stonework. They are elegant and moving in their simple elegy to the lost generations.

In front of a sandstone wall stands a bronze statue—a winged woman crowned with a laurel wreath and carrying a palm frond. It was described as an 'Emblematic Figure of Peace' at

1924

Nelson Street, Lancaster
Grid Reference: SD 47908 61530
Listed Building Grade II

the unveiling ceremony, but is known more commonly as 'Victory' (the Greek goddess Nike). To either side of the figure, under the inscription that reads: IN HONOURED MEMORY OF THE MEN OF LANCASTER WHO GAVE THEIR LIVES IN THE GREAT WAR 1914–1919, are tall recessed panels of bronze, bearing the names of more than 1000 men (including sixty-three sets of brothers) who died. These panels were unveiled at the ceremony by the mothers of men who had died in the First World War. In front of the statue is a stone tomb-chest flanked by square bronze vases. These bear the names of over 300 who died in the Second World War and in the Korean War. On the front of the tomb-chest is cut a further inscription: 1939 : 1945 AND OTHER CONFLICTS.

The memorial was designed by Thomas Mawson and Sons, a prominent firm of local landscape architects who attained international acclaim for their work. Among his achievements, Thomas Hayton Mawson (1861-1933) became president of the Town and Planning Institute, as well as the first president of the newly formed Institute of Landscape Architects. His published work of 1901, *The Art and Craft of Garden Making,* is widely accepted as the foundation of modern landscape architecture.[29] The company offices were located in a large Georgian building on High Street, and are commemorated there by a plaque.

IN HONOURED MEMORY OF THE MEN OF
LANCASTER WHO GAVE THEIR LIVES
IN THE GREAT WAR 1914-1919
1939 : 1945 AND OTHER CONFLICTS

John Stirzaker, Market Gardener

We take our final letter from the gravestone, not of the many, but of the one: that of John Stirzaker, aged just twenty-one at his death in 1845. This curious surname is derived from the Old Norse personal name 'Styrr', and the word for ploughed field, 'akr'; hence, 'Styrr's akr'. The name has a strong location connection with the nearby parish of Garstang, and there were many Stirzakers recorded as living in the area during the Nineteenth century. These

1845

Castle Hill, Lancaster
Grid Reference: SD 47295 61966

IN MEMORY OF
JOHN STIRZAKER,
SON OF JOHN AND
JANE STIRZAKER,
WHO DIED ON
AUGUST 13TH 1845
AGED 21 YEARS

included mariners, engine tenders, land owners, mill workers, gardeners and transported convicts. Further back, we even find Robert Stirzaker, Mayor of Lancaster in 1686.

John was born on 16th January 1824, and was baptised in the Priory church a hundred yards from where his gravestone now lies. His parents, John and Jane (née Clark) lived in Back Lane off Penny Street, along with John's two brothers and a sister. By the age of seventeen, John had followed his father into the family trade of market gardening. Later, the family moved to Milking Style Lane and then on to Meeting House Lane.[30]

One interesting detail from the census data is the variation in the spelling of the family name, from Stirzaker in 1841, to Sterzaher (1851) and then Sterzaker (1861). This was not an uncommon occurrence when the details were open, not only to interpretation by the census collector, but to different spelling variations among family members.

His gravestone, along with many others, was moved from its original location in the nearby graveyard and laid flat to form an amphitheatre that leads down from the Priory on Castle Hill. The inscription is v-cut into the gravestone, and in some cases, such as the letter Z, the upper and lower horizontal bars are separated from the diagonals, creating what is almost a stencil effect. The letters are simple and elegant, and almost invisible, slight depressions in an unremarkable slab of grey rock. But preserved in the stone, they present the opportunity to explore the city's past through the lives of those who once lived and worked in its streets and lanes.

There are still Stirzaker's living in the Lancaster area today.

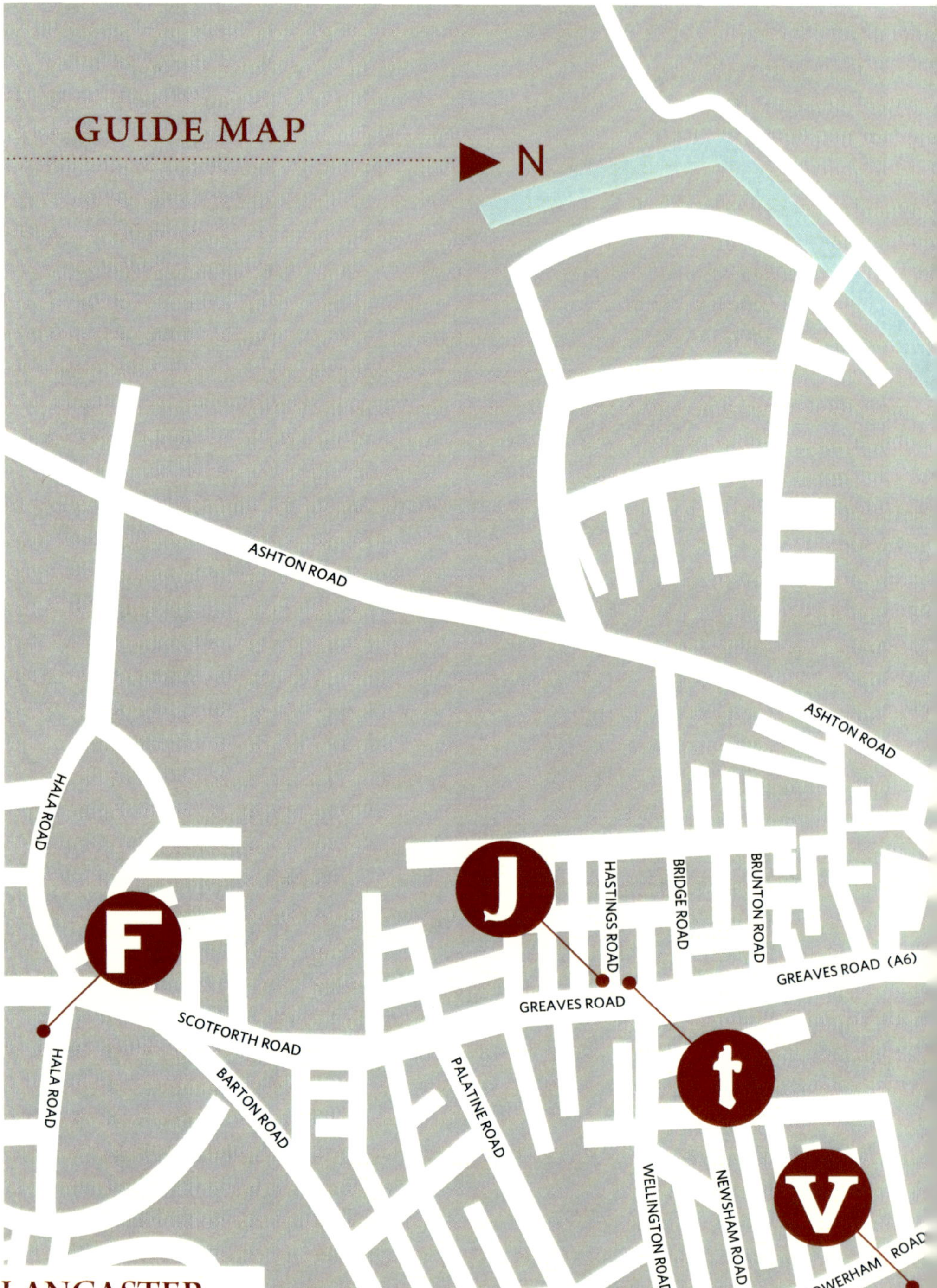
GUIDE MAP
N
ASHTON ROAD
ASHTON ROAD
HALA ROAD
HALA ROAD
F
J
t
V
HASTINGS ROAD
BRIDGE ROAD
BRUNTON ROAD
GREAVES ROAD (A6)
GREAVES ROAD
SCOTFORTH ROAD
BARTON ROAD
PALATINE ROAD
WELLINGTON ROAD
NEWSHAM ROAD
BOWERHAM ROAD
LANCASTER

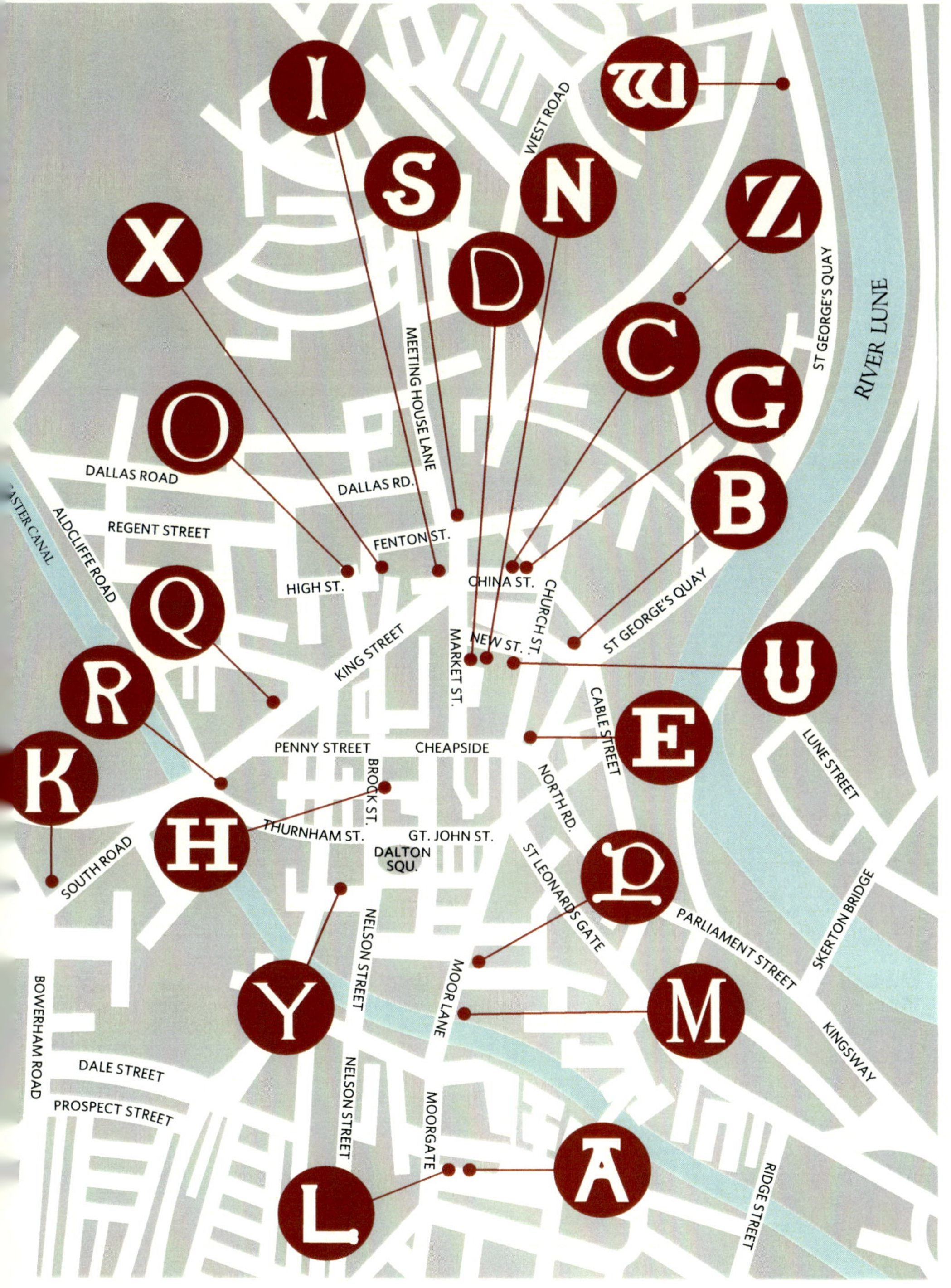

RIVER LUNE
ST GEORGE'S QUAY
WEST ROAD
MEETING HOUSE LANE
DALLAS ROAD
DALLAS RD.
REGENT STREET
FENTON ST.
ALDCLIFFE ROAD
HIGH ST.
CHINA ST.
CHURCH ST.
ST GEORGE'S QUAY
KING STREET
MARKET ST.
NEW ST.
CABLE STREET
PENNY STREET
CHEAPSIDE
BROCK ST.
NORTH RD.
LUNE STREET
THURNHAM ST.
GT. JOHN ST.
DALTON SQU.
SOUTH ROAD
ST LEONARDS GATE
SKERTON BRIDGE
PARLIAMENT STREET
NELSON STREET
MOOR LANE
KINGSWAY
BOWERHAM ROAD
DALE STREET
PROSPECT STREET
NELSON STREET
MOORGATE
RIDGE STREET

GLOSSARY

Aedicule: an opening or niche, framed by columns on either side, and with a pediment above.

Ampersand: a conflation of the phrase 'and per se and', that represents the word 'and'.

Arabesque: artistic decoration that consists of patterns of intertwining and flowing lines: originally found in Arabic or Moorish design.

Arcade: a covered walk enclosed by a line of arches on one or both sides.

Arm: a horizontal or upward sloping stroke of a letter that connects to a stem or stoke at only one end.

Art Deco: artistic and design style originating in Paris in the 1920s. It emphasised elegance, functionality, symmetry and modernity.

Arts & Crafts: international design movement existent mainly between 1860 and 1910. It was led by the artist William Morris (1834–1896) and architect Charles Voysey (1857–1941), and was influenced by the writings of Ruskin (1819–1900) and Pugin (1812–1852). It emphasised traditional craftsmanship, often employing decorative medieval, romantic or folk styles.

Ashlar: dressed stonework with square edges and smooth faces.

Baseline: imaginary line upon which most letters appear to sit and below which descenders extend.

Bays: a unit of form in architecture. Usually the area between columns or pilasters; or that within a window frame or door frame.

Bar: the horizontal stroke of a letter (also known as a crossbar).

Bifurcated: where the terminal stem of a letter is divided in two.

Blackletter: a letterform with contrasting thick-and-thin, angular strokes forming upright letterforms. Also known as Gothic.

Bowl: curved part of a character enclosing the circular counter of some letters.

Canted: part of a façade which is at an angle to another part of the same façade. The angle being less than a right angle.

Capital: the crowning part of a column or pilaster.

Clarendon: a slab-serif typeface created in England by Robert Besley around 1838.

Cornice: a horizontal moulded projection that sits atop a building.

Counter: the enclosed or partially enclosed space of some letters such as D, P, O, and S.

Course: a continuous horizontal layer of similarly-sized building material, usually in a wall.

(String) Course: a projecting course of brickwork or stone that runs horizontally around a building.

Cursive: lettering simulating handwriting.

Descender: the portion of a lowercase letter that extends below the baseline.

Doric: an order of architecture characterised by, among other features, smooth, round capitals that are simple and plain.

Eaves: the lower edges of a roof that usually project beyond the walls of the building to carry rainwater away.

Engrave: to carve, cut, or etch a design or letters into a surface.

Entablature: mouldings and bands that lie horizontally above columns, and resting on their capitals.

Finial: a decorative device used to emphasise the apex of a gable.

Frieze: a wide central band, either plain or decorated, set on the face of a building or wall.

Gable: the part of the front or side of a building enclosed by the end of a pitched roof.

(Dutch) Gable: a gable with sides made up of one or more curves and having a pediment.

Georgian: architectural styles developed between 1720 and 1840 and characterised by proportion and symmetry, where simple ratios determine the dimensions of architectural features and their relationship to each other.

Gothic: a style of architecture often defined by its pointed arches, vaulted buttresses, large windows, and spires.

Gritstone: a porous sedimentary rock composed of coarse, often angular sand grains.

Incised: cut or engraved into a surface.

Ionic: an order of classical architecture where columns have scrolls that are set over the front and rear parts of the column capitals.

Jacobean Revival: an architectural style made popular in England from the late 1820s, and combining elements of Elizabethan and Jacobean architectural styles.

Leg: the lower, descending stroke of letters K and

R, as well as the tail of the Q.

Modernist: a style of architecture associated with the late Nineteenth and early Twentieth centuries, and characterised by simplification of form and ornamentation.

Monoline: lettering where strokes are uniform.

Moulded: a strip of material with various cross sections used for decoration.

Mullion: a vertical structural element that divides adjacent window units, acting primarily as a structural support to an arch or lintel above the window opening.

Northern Renaissance: architectural style emphasising symmetry, proportion and geometry, as demonstrated in the architecture of classical antiquity and in particular ancient Rome.

Oculus: a circular or oval window.

Oriel: a bay window.

Pediment: the triangular section found above the horizontal structure (entablature), and usually supported by columns.

(Segmental) Pediment: where the pediment is in the form of a segment of a circle, rather than a triangle.

(Scrolled) Pediment: an open-topped curved pediment, where its two S-shaped sides end in scrolls.

Pilaster: a projecting column built into or applied to the face of a wall. Most are commonly flattened or rectangular in form.

Purlin: a horizontal structural member that supports the roof.

Quoin: the cornerstones of brick or stone walls.

Relief: a technique where the impression is given that the sculpted material has been raised above the background surface.

Roman: a form of lettering with thick and thin strokes terminating in serifs.

Royal Cipher: a monogram-like device of a country's reigning sovereign, typically consisting of the initials of the monarch's name and title, and often surmounted by a crown.

Rustication: textured exterior wall features that contrast with the smoothly finished, squared block masonry surfaces called ashlar.

(Banded) Rustication: where bands of textured exterior ornamentation alternate with smooth ashlar stonework.

San Serif: a letter without serifs.

Sandstone: a sedimentary rock composed mainly of sand-sized minerals or rock grains.

Segmental Head: an arch formed by a segment of a circle, less than a semi-circle, and often much flatter.

Serif: semi-structural details on the ends of the strokes that make up letters, often in the form of decorative lines.

(Bracketed) Serif: a curved or wedge-like connection between the stem of a letter and the serif.

(Slab) Serif: serifs that are thick or block-like.

(Slur) Serif: serifs that are rounded and unbracketed.

Sill: a shelf or slab at the foot of a window or doorway.

Stem: the main, usually vertical stroke of a letter.

Strapwork: decorative ornamentation consisting of strips or bands cut into elaborate shapes, with piercings and often interwoven.

Stroke: the main diagonal part of a letterform such as in N, M, or Y.

Terminal: the end of any stroke of a letter.

Textura: a form of Blackletter text that has calligraphic characteristics.

Transitional: typefaces that have characteristics that include marked contrast between thick and thin strokes, more upright stress in letters and serifs that tend towards horizontal.

Transom: a horizontal member separating a door from a window or fanlight above it.

Truss: a straight member connected at joints and composed of triangular units.

Tuscan: a classical order of architecture with limited ornamentations. Where applied to architectural lettering, it refers to embellishments including bulges on stems and strokes, or split terminals.

Vaulted: an arched structure, usually of masonry, and covering a space.

V-cut: incised letters which have a v-shaped section.

Victorian: architectural styles employed predominantly during the middle and late Nineteenth century.

Voussoir: a wedge-shaped element, typically a stone used in building an arch or vault.

SOURCES OF INFORMATION

PUBLICATIONS

1. Bland, G. M. (1932) A Brief Description of the Library Movement in Lancaster, in R. M. Middleton *Official Opening of the Central Public Library*, pp.11-12: Borough of Lancaster.
2. Bull, S. (2007) *Triumphant Rider: The Lancaster Roman Cavalry Tombstone*: Palatine Books, Lancaster.
3. Fleury, C. (1891) *Time-honoured Lancaster: Historic notes on the ancient borough of Lancaster*: Eaton & Bulfield Printers, Lancaster.
4. Garnet, E. (1994) *The Dated Buildings of South Lonsdale*: Folio, Lancaster University.
5. Gregg, G. (1977) *Schools and Education in Lancaster: A Brief Outline*: Lancaster Museum Monograph, Lancaster.
6. Irving, R. (1987) *Lancaster Past and Present*. Neil Richardson, Manchester.
7. Irving, R. (1988) *More Lancaster Past and Present*. Neil Richardson, Manchester.
8. Lancashire County Council (2006) *Lancashire Historic Town Survey Programme: Lancaster Historic Town Assessment Report*. Lancashire County Council.
9. Lancaster Education Committee (1925) *Education Week Handbook, October 11-17*: Lancaster Guardian, Lancaster.
10. Lancashire Historic Environment Record, Lancashire County Council.
11. Lowe, E. H. (n. d.) *Methodism in Lancaster*. Unpublished: Lancaster City Library, Lancaster.
12. Mosley, J. (1999) *The Nymph and the Grot*: Friends of St Bride Printing Library, London.
13. Müller, S. (2008): *The name Odd Fellows, from Concept and Contents of Odd Fellowship, in The Independent Order of Odd Fellows*. 'Cultural Studies in the Heartland of America' project, Wissenschaftlicher Verlag, Trier.
14. Price, J. (1998) *Sharpe, Paley and Austin: A Lancaster Architectural Practice 1836-1942*: CNWRS, Lancaster University
15. Price, J. (1989) *Industrial Lancaster*. Local Studies No.12: Lancaster City Museum, Lancaster.
16. Robinson, A. (1880) *A Concise History of the Independent United Order of Mechanics Friendly Societies, from 1847 to 1879*: John B. Barnes, Newcastle-on-Tyne.
17. Snoek, J. (2008) *Ritual Dynamics in the Independent United Order of Mechanics*: Forums Ritualdynamik, Heidelberg.
18. Trades Directories [Accessed from Lancashire Records Office and from Lancaster Community History Library].
19. Tyson, E. (Ed.) (1982) *Schools and Education in Lancaster*: Lancaster Museums Monograph, Lancaster.
20. Wade, P. (n.d.) *Lancaster's Nineteenth Century Scientific Legacy*: Lancaster Museums, Lancaster.
21. White, A. (2003) *Lancaster: A History*: Phillimore Ltd, West Sussex.
22. White, A. and Winstanley, M. (1996) *Victorian Terrace Houses in Lancaster*: CNWRS, University of Lancaster.
23. Wilson, S. (ed.) (2002) *Aspects of Lancaster*: Wharcliffe Books, Barnsley.
24. Winstanley, M. (2001) The Town Transformed, 1815-1914. In: *A History of Lancaster*. Andrew White, ed. Edinburgh University Press, Edinburgh, pp.173-228.

WEBSITES AND ONLINE RESOURCES

25. Lancaster City Council. [online] Available at: http://www.lancaster.gov.uk/council-and-democracy/civic-ceremonial/lord-ashton-lino-king/ [Accessed 20 August 2011].
26. *The London Gazette*, 10th October, 1882. [online] Available at: http://www.london-gazette.co.uk/issues/25155/pages/4597/page.pdf [Accessed 22 October 2011].
27. Tatham History Society *Reminiscences of life in Victorian rural Lancashire*. [online] Available at: http://www.tathamhistory.org.uk/tdsmith.php> [Accessed 18 December 2011].
28. Greenlane Archaeology Ltd 2009 *Pye Warehouse, Fleet Square, Lancaster, Lancashire: Archaeology Watching Brief*. [online] Available at: http://archaeologydataservice.ac.uk/catalogue/adsdata/arch-700-1/dissemination/pdf/greenlan1-71297_1.pdf [Accessed 12 October 2011].
29. *Visit Cumbria* Thomas Hayton Mawson (1861-1933.) [online] Available at: http://www.visitcumbria.com/thomas-mawson.htm [Accessed 02 February2012].
30. England and Wales Census Data. [online] Available at: http://www.ancestry.co.uk/, from Lancaster Community History Library.

LIBRARIES, MUSEUMS AND ARCHIVES

Lancashire Records Office, Bow Lane, Preston, Lancashire, PR1 2RE.

Lancaster City Museum, Market Square, Lancaster, LA1 1HT.

Lancaster Community Heritage Centre, New Street, Lancaster, LA1 1EG.

FURTHER READING

Baines, P & Dixon. C. (2008) *Signs: Lettering in the Environment*: Laurence King, London.

Bartram, A. (2007) *Typeforms: A History*: Oak Knoll Press and The British Library, London.

Bartram, A. (1978) *Lettering in Architecture*: Lund Humphries, Bradford, London.

Bartram, A. (1975) *Street Name Lettering in the British Isles*: Lund Humphries, London.

Gray, N. (1986) *A History of Lettering*: Phaidon Press.

Gray, N. (1960) *Lettering on Buildings*: Architectural Press, London.

Kinneir, J. (1980) *Words and Buildings: The art and practice of public lettering,* Architectural Press, London.

THIS STONE WAS LAID BY HIS
ORSHIP THE MAYOR COUNCILLOR
INSON JP JUNE 9TH 1931
PARR CHAIRMAN THIS
SUBSCRIPT
ESTABLIS
VICE AND

ACKNOWLEDGEMENTS

I would like to express my thanks to Bev Kain, Mick Murphy and Jonathan Westaway for their encouragement, advice and support in the development of this publication. Also, to Peter Iles, Specialist Advisor (Archaeology) at Lancashire County Council, for providing key details about a number of the buildings given in this work. In addition, I would like to thank Cultural Services at Lancashire County Council for permission to include details from historic documents. The Cultural Services Team, Lancashire County Records Office and Lancashire Libraries and Museums, remain invaluable sources of information, expertise and research, and I would like to extend my admiration and thanks for the work they do in preserving and enhancing the heritage of Lancaster and the County of Lancashire. Finally, I would like to thank Mick Murphy for his permission to use the poem *Passage West*, which is incorporated into the lettering map of Lancaster on pages 56-57.

Simon Hawkesworth

Lancaster

2012